W9-CIQ-852

PERGAMON INTERNATIONAL LIBRARY
of Science, Technology, Engineering and Social Studies

*The 1000-volume original paperback library in aid of education,
industrial training and the enjoyment of leisure*

Publisher: Robert Maxwell, M.C.

ESSAYS ON PLANNING THEORY
AND EDUCATION

THE PERGAMON TEXTBOOK
INSPECTION COPY SERVICE

An inspection copy of any book published in the Pergamon International Library will
gladly be sent to academic staff without obligation for their consideration for course
adoption or recommendation. Copies may be retained for a period of 60 days from
receipt and returned if not suitable. When a particular title is adopted or recommended
for adoption for class use and the recommendation results in a sale of 12 or more copies,
the inspection copy may be retained with our compliments. The Publishers will be
pleased to receive suggestions for revised editions and new titles to be published in this
important International Library.

ESSAYS ON PLANNING THEORY AND EDUCATION

ANDREAS FALUDI Dipl-Ing, Dr techn

Professor of Planning, University of Amsterdam,
formerly Delft University of Technology and Oxford Polytechnic

PERGAMON PRESS

OXFORD · NEW YORK · TORONTO · SYDNEY
PARIS · FRANKFURT

U. K.	Pergamon Press Ltd., Headington Hill Hall, Oxford OX3 0BW, England
U. S. A.	Pergamon Press Inc., Maxwell House, Fairview Park, Elmsford, New York 10523, U.S.A.
C A N A D A	Pergamon of Canada Ltd., 75 The East Mall, Toronto, Ontario, Canada
A U S T R A L I A	Pergamon Press (Aust.) Pty. Ltd., 19a Boundary Street, Rushcutters Bay, N.S.W. 2011, Australia
F R A N C E	Pergamon Press SARL, 24 rue des Ecoles, 75240 Paris, Cedex 05, France
F E D E R A L REPUBLIC OF GERMANY	Pergamon Press GmbH, 6242 Kronberg-Taunus, Pferdstrasse 1, Federal Republic of Germany

First edition 1978

British Library Cataloguing in Publication Data

Faludi, Andreas
Essays on planning theory and education.
1. City planning – Study and teaching
2. Regional planning – Study and teaching
I. Title
711'.07'11   HT165.5   77-30343
ISBN 0-08-021224-7 (Hardcase)
ISBN 0-08-021223-9 (Flexicover)

Printed in Great Britain by A. Wheaton & Co., Ltd., Exeter

Contents

v

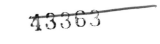

Acknowledgements

My thanks are due to the editors and publishers of the original versions of the essays contained in this volume for their kind permission to reprint. "Planning Education: A European View of British Experience" was first published in the proceedings of the Fourth Salzburg Congress of Urban Planning and Development (SCUPAD) organised by the alumni organisation of the urban planning courses of the Salzburg Seminar of American Studies in 1969. "The 'Specialist' versus 'Generalist' Conflict 1963–5" is an excerpt from Number 12 of the *Oxford Working Papers in Planning Education and Research* (The "Specialist" versus "Generalist" Conflict) published by the Department of Town Planning of the Oxford Polytechnic in 1972. "British Planning Education: the Changing Scene" is an excerpt from Number 7 of the *Working Papers in Planning Theory and Education* (The Social Sciences in the Planning Curriculum) published by the Vereniging voor Studien Studentenbelangen te Delft at Delft University of Technology in 1975. "Teaching the Planning Process" was originally published in the *Journal of the Royal Town Planning Institute* (Vol. 58, No. 3, March 1972). "Action Space Analysis" comes out of Number 8 of the above mentioned *Working Papers in Planning Theory and Education* published in 1975. "The Experiences of Sociologists in their Collaboration with Planners" was an address to a Planning & Transport Research & Computation Co. Ltd. (PTRC) seminar and published in the proceedings *Uses of Social Science in Urban Planning* in 1971. "The Position of Sociologists in Planning Schools" is an excerpt of Number 4 of the above mentioned *Oxford Working Papers in Planning Education and Research* (Sociology in Planning Education) published in 1970. "Sociology in Planning Education" was first published in *Urban Studies* (Vol. 13, No. 2, June 1976). "Planning Theory and the Education of Planners" has never been published in English. Its Dutch version came out under the title *Planningtheorie en planningonderwijs* in 1975. The publisher was Delft University Press.

Naturally, with a collection of essays written over a period of several years, many individuals have contributed through giving me their direct assistance. Space does not permit to name them all. Anyhow, my memory might fail me in recounting them all. My thanks are due to them nevertheless, and I can only hope that they will accept them in this summary fashion.

In compiling this volume of essays, I have received valuable guidance from the Editorial Board of Pergamon's Urban and Regional Planning Series, and in particular from Mr. Brian Styles who has read and commented on the manuscript on their behalf. As often before in the two-and-a-half fruitful years of direct collaboration, Mr. Stephen L. Hamnett has made perceptive remarks on the final two papers and on the various introductory texts and contributed through patient editing of their English.

Most of these essays have been written whilst at the Department of Town Planning of the Oxford Polytechnic. I wish my colleagues amongst staff and successive generations of students to know that I think of these years as a particularly happy period of my life, and one that was fruitful in terms of the intellectual exchanges taking place. My thanks are due to all of them for their friendship and stimulation of which they gave so freely.

Last but not least my wife deserves mention for her support which continued during the years when these essays were written right up until the present, when compiling this volume yet again demanded sacrifices of the kind she cheerfully accepts as part of our life.

Andreas Faludi
Delft

Introduction

This volume should give evidence of a continuing interest in the twin fields of planning theory and education. It succeeds two previous ones: *A Reader in Planning Theory* (Faludi, 1973a) and *Planning Theory* (Faludi, 1973b), both of which are primarily designed to meet educational needs without being concerned with educational matters as such. It is hoped that an account of the *joint* evolution of thought in both these fields will add to the understanding of planning theory as a conceptual basis for planning and engender discussion of and improvements to the education of planners.

The two fields are indeed closely related. Planning education raises theoretical issues even more directly than practice. Without its growth, planning theory would hardly have become the area of active intellectual pursuit which it is today. The essays in this volume describe challenges and responses during this development.

Naturally, any selection of essays written by one and the same author over an extensive period of time will reflect his personal biography. I landed, more or less accidentally, in the world of British town planning education at a time when it was about to embark on a development unknown hitherto. Britain was indeed a kind of dream world for planning education in the late sixties. For reasons described in the first essays in this volume, the demand for, and the opportunities in, planning education were plentiful and the setting favourable. The Department of Town Planning of the Oxford Polytechnic which I joined was itself a child of this expansionary situation and its development symptomatic of the growth of planning education in Britain.

One of the significant factors during this period was the sympathetic attitude of the then Town Planning Institute towards undergraduate planning education. This was in contrast to earlier scepticism which, incidentally, is still widespread, especially outside Britain. In the United States with an admittedly different structure of higher education, there has never been much discussion of it, and few courses are known to follow this pattern. On the Continent, a mere handful of courses exists which one might conceivably compare with the British model, but most of them are of recent origin and any judgement on them must be premature.[1]

I profess myself a supporter of undergraduate planning education (though not to the exclusion of other models such as graduate courses). But my reasons are different from those that led the Town Planning Institute to favour it in the late sixties. As the first papers in this volume should demonstrate, its reasons largely stemmed from professional interests. The example of the undergraduate courses at the University of Manchester, and the educational arguments advanced by its head, then Chairman of the Education Committee of the Town Planning Institute, certainly helped. But on the whole, educational arguments played very little part in bringing undergraduate planning education about.

My reasons, by contrast, are educational and theoretical. Firstly I have always been convinced that good undergraduate courses can be devised, and developments in Britain since the early seventies have generally borne me out. Some dead wood has been cut out of courses making room for new inputs, in particular from the social sciences whose role concerns me in three essays towards the end of this volume. Of its architectural inheritance, generally, only project work has remained as a prominent feature of planning education, a point to which I shall return later in this introduction. But even here, the drawing-board syndrome and the burning of midnight oil to get laborious designs ready for next day's "crit" have given way to a pattern of work more reminiscent of today's practice with its predominance of typewriters, photocopying machines and working party meetings.

Above all, undergraduate planning education poses the greater challenge for planning theory. The intellectual adventure which fascinates me most is the following: If, as my previous works have argued strongly, and as the

[1]A notable exception is the four-year course offered at the University of Dortmund. Through the agencies of Gerd Albers, himself well acquainted with British planning education and practice, British educational thinking appears to have played its part in bringing this development about. Delft University of Technology offers a course which shows some similarity but without having been much influenced by Britain. The University of Technology of Vienna is experimenting with an undergraduate course, but it is still early days for assessing its success.

final essay in this volume restates, there is a useful distinction to be drawn between procedural and substantial theory in planning, the former being generic to various kinds of purposive action and the latter focusing the former on a particular area of concern, then there are interesting consequences to be drawn for education. This is because, seen from this point of view, town planning becomes but *one* of the fields of application of a generic planning approach. The *teaching* of town planning might similarly be conceived as the teaching of this approach through its *application to one particular field. Planning Theory* on a town planning course is then mainly concerned with town planning as a *manifestation of the planning approach*.

Better still, and this takes the argument one step further into the realm of speculation about the future, the planning approach and its theoretical base might form the object of study of a truly "generalist" *course on planning as such*. This would then be followed by a variety of "specialist" courses on its application to various planning fields, town planning being one of them.

In this way, undergraduate planning education might shed its specific links with town planning and attempt to educate men and women for practical effectiveness in a great many fields, an effectiveness which requires forethought, judgement and determination in seeing projects through. They would naturally have to acquire detailed knowledge of their particular field of action but this would come only *after* the teaching of planning as a skill, but above all as a manner of thinking, as such. (To be sure, practical problems would always figure prominently in the type of course proposed, but only by way of *example* and not in order to learn about them as such.)

Such is the logic of Perloff's "generalist-with-a-specialism" model of a course extended to incorporate fields other than town planning. It figures prominently in various of the papers in this volume. Admittedly, it fits British and American higher education with its two-tier degree structure more readily than higher education elsewhere. Thus, the penultimate paper outlines an undergraduate "Planning Studies" course which might be followed by a variety of postgraduate courses focusing planning approaches and skills on various areas of concern, and which it might be conceivable to implement in a British planning school. But there is nothing to prevent courses elsewhere from being given an internal structure on the lines of this model. Degrees and certificates at set points are not essential to its logic.

The final essay picks up this point and expands it in outlining possible implications of this model for education generally in today's and tomorrow's world. Since practical effectiveness coupled with the ability for theoretical reflection which form the essence of planning education are becoming increasingly important in nearly every field, I can envisage them as prominent features of future adult and even secondary education, as well as university courses aimed at increasing the relevance of their teaching to practical life. An essential element of this model which receives attention in various essays in this volume is project work as a central educational vehicle. Again, my arguments concerning project work in *town* planning education should count as exemplary for arguments concerning planning education as such.

As mentioned before, project work in *town* planning education stems from its architectural heritage. It is characterised by the attempt to tackle problems similar to those encountered in practice. Since architectural practice used to centre around individual design work, it was easy enough to make project work resemble it by handing out design briefs.

In a way, project work in early architecture and town planning education was nothing more than a continuation of an even older tradition: apprenticeship, the more so as student-pupils frequently worked on projects of their masters. Certainly, project work of this kind emerged independently from educational considerations of the advantages of learning by doing and self-guidance which permeate recent discussions of the reform of higher education.[2]

However, the problems which town planners face nowadays, the context within which they find themselves, and their methods of work have changed. Town planning is firmly recognised as being ultimately concerned with the promotion and control of development through the application of the force of law on the one hand and the purposive expenditure of public funds on the other. This places the town planner in the public sphere, with all the ensuing consequences of being affected by whatever crises society and its institutions might be in, and becoming

---

[2]See, for instance, Fortuin (1974) for a report on the Dutch situation. Crispin (1975) gives a review of the British literature.

unavoidably concerned with the legitimacy of state action. In all these respects, his position coincides with that of other policy experts, and cooperation and conflict with these, as with many other participants in the complex game of getting things done, are his daily bread.

With these changes the traditional form of project work has become sorely inadequate as an educational vehicle for preparing for practice. There is a variety of roles for planners, many of them involving skills different from design. Alongside these *cognitive* skills planners must also have social skills. Success or failure in planning often depend as much on the competent management of a network of relations as on the depth of analysis on which plans are based, as Friedmann (1973) and Friend *et al.* (1974) remind us. Project briefs must therefore be specific on the roles in which they cast planners and on the web of inter-active relationships which link them via their proposals to their multi-faceted clientele. As the fourth paper "Teaching the Planning Process" shows this can usefully be done, in basic planning teaching in any case, through some process of simulation. The sense of realism which they are quite capable of achieving apart, the elements of complexity and uncertainty introduced by such devices into project work, are necessary for theoretical and educational reasons: how else could one teach process planning, the need for flexibility and for reducing unnecessary commitment which are the hall-marks of recent planning thought but by making students *experience* situations similar to those which have brought the need for those approaches about, situations which create information overload and thus anxiety, and require amongst other things skills in handling them.

My stance on the themes raised above of support for the idea of undergraduate planning education, of planning theory as an intellectual core of planning curricula and project work, albeit of a specific type, as its main educational vehicle, and my concern for the role of the social sciences and social scientists in their development, did not change much during the period covered by the essays in this volume. Its structure reflects these stable elements in my thinking. After a section describing "The British Planning Education Scene", it goes straight to a section on educational practice ("From the Work-bench of Planning Education") showing by way of example how project work can be used to teach aspects of planning theory. The following part delves deeper into theoretical issues raised in considering "Sociology in Planning Education", summarising ideas concerning the generalist-with-a-specialism model in a way which is consistent with the attitude outlined above of regarding town planning as an (exemplary) field of application of a generic planning approach.

The "Synthesis" part finally contains only one paper: my inaugural lecture held at Delft University of Technology with which I aimed to summarise my earlier experiences and to focus them on a new and sometimes bewildering problem: planning education in an environment where even town planning as known in Britain is neither very easy to identify as an activity nor very sure of being recognised as such. Naturally, I hope that the synthesis of my first year-and-a-half at Delft will be followed by new explorations, but this is for the future to decide and the synthesis thus represents where I stand at present.

There are also points on which my views have changed since publishing the first of these essays and it is to these that I shall turn. For reasons indicated above, the undergraduate *versus* graduate debate in Britain, although relevant because of the issues concerning planning which it raises, cannot be related directly to the situation of planning education in the Netherlands. The only course which, with suitable modifications, might conceivably emulate the undergraduate model is at Delft University of Technology where I taught until recently. However, debates in the Faculty of Architecture and Planning there concentrate more on the relation between the two than on the development of the field of town planning and on planning education as such. In this environment, talk about shaping a curriculum on planning as a generic activity forming the basis for the application of planning skills to a variety of fields seems rather far fetched. So, out of necessity, although still present in my inaugural lecture, the issue has somewhat receded into the background.

Secondly, there is less debate taking place in my new environment about planning educational matters generally, a point to which I shall return in due course. This means that there is not the same amount of purposive discussion aimed at identifying conceptual links between subjects, and thus the hub around which a curriculum should revolve, as was the case during the period covered by these essays. The notion of planning theory as an essential element of the core of the planning curriculum therefore has less meaning and also recedes into the background. Planning theory is rather seen as on *a par* with other inputs.

A change which antecedes my coming to the Netherlands concerns life projects. The first paper suggests that students should go out into the community and tackle problems that matter to some of the people there. Little did I know about the difficulties which this generates, not the least for "the people", and on which nowadays some experience exists. Although I would never deny that such projects might fulfil a useful function in the curriculum and for educational institutions concerned about their relations with the outside world, I am now very firmly convinced that a laboratory-type setting with simulated partners is more apposite for *basic* teaching of planning approaches and skills. Life projects are almost as difficult to plan ahead as life is, and thus tend to play havoc with the curriculum. Considerations of sheer effectiveness of curriculum planning, i.e. the mutual reinforcement of parallel and successive courses on which so much depends in education, are therefore powerful arguments in favour of the more limited simulation formula, in early years in any case.

Closely related to this question is the amount of self-guidance which is often seen as the hall-mark of project work in higher education generally. The first essay in this volume again advocates this principle and broadly speaking for the same reasons as are generally advanced in its favour. However, self-guidance, in particular in the selection of problems to be tackled, tends to prevent projects from being adequately prepared. In particular, integration with the rest of the curriculum regularly suffers. Here, a classic trade-off situation exists therefore, and I am for recognising this as such. Compromises can usually be found nevertheless. For instance, through careful design and handling of the project, choices can be built into them, but within an overall framework set by the project co-ordinator for which he must take responsibility.

Another change antedating my coming to the Netherlands concerns a philosophical point: my views concerning ambiguity in education. The first essay strikes a note of intolerance with ambiguity, especially where the role of the social sciences and of theory are concerned. Since then, however, I have had to live with continuous ambiguity, and the move back to the Continent has certainly not changed this. I would like to think that I have even come to value it positively, if for no other reason than because it generates intellectual tension in efforts to resolve it whilst knowing that, of necessity, ambiguity of some kind will always remain.

Lastly, I have softened on yet another count, i.e. my appreciation of the role of the Royal Town Planning Institute. Whilst always recognising the part which it had played in bringing the dreamland of planning education about of which I wrote in the first paragraphs of this introduction, I was also largely critical of what I perceived as the retarding influence of the professional body on the realisation of perceived future possibilities. However, in later years, and especially since coming to Holland, I have become more appreciative of the Royal Town Planning Institute for having created a forum for planning education debate.

As stated in the beginning, this volume hopes to engender such debate, not only in Britain, but also abroad, and hopefully also more exchanges of ideas between planning educators of various countries. Variations notwithstanding, there are broad similarities in the problems they face, problems which can only increase as time goes by, unless vigorous efforts are taken to overcome them. There is in particular bound to be disenchantment with planning and its apparent failure to deal with present day crises. As one of its consequences there is bound to be equally great disenchantment within the profession faced with alienated clients. This might focus on the apparent futility of all the soul-searching and academic theorising that has gone on during the past years. There will be an urgent call for immediate relevance to the professional jobs of practitioners, instead of to the fundamental issues mankind is faced with as perceived through academic eyes. It will be the task of planning educators to meet justified demands for the relevance of teaching to professional practice, and simultaneously to stand their ground on the need for enough autonomy for education to allow for theoretical reflection. Only in this way will planners be *educated* instead of merely trained for practice.

References

CRISPIN, G. (1975) Project work in education for urban and regional planning, *Working Papers in Planning Theory and Education*, No. 4, Vereniging voor Studie-en Studentenbelangen te Delft.

FALUDI, A. (1973a) *A Reader in Planning Theory*, Pergamon, Oxford.

FALUDI, A. (1973b) *Planning Theory*, Pergamon, Oxford.

FORTUIN, S. (1974) *Handleiding voor projektonderwijs*, Stichting Inter-universitaire Instituut voor Social-Wetenschappelijk Onderzoek, Amsterdam.

FRIEDMANN, J. (1973) *Retracking America*, Doubleday, New York.

FRIEND, J. K. *et al.* (1974) *Public Planning – the inter-corporate Dimension*, Tavistock, London.

Part I

The British Planning Education Scene

This section comprises three papers which, between them, should allow the reader to appreciate the interactive development of the planning profession and planning education in Britain. Two of them, the first and the third, were written for a largely non-British audience: the first (my first essay on planning theory and education) as a paper given at the fourth Salzburg Congress in Urban Planning and Development held in 1969. Although it has been slightly edited, it retains the flavour of an address. As against this, the third essay was first published some years afterwards. It comes out of one of the *Working Papers in Planning Theory and Education* published by the Planning Theory Group at Delft University of Technology to engender discussion in these twin fields which thus continue to attract my keen interest.

As against these two essays, the second one (coming out of one of the *Oxford Working Papers in Planning Education and Research*) analyses one particular, though very important, episode in the development of British town planning in considerable detail. Although it proved necessary to interpose it between the first and the last (after all, it explains certain points made in the first essay in more detail, and the historical line of development sketched by it is taken much further by the third dealing with developments after this episode), the non-British reader might profitably read the introductory paragraphs to the third paper before turning to the second.

Apart from forming the basis for an understanding of the British planning education scene, these papers also introduce essential features of my thinking on planning theory and education. The first paper in particular outlines an intellectual programme which is still guiding much of my thoughts and actions. Likewise, the remaining papers have as underlying themes certain aspects of this programme. All three essays are offered in the hope that their arguments are of continuing relevance. Thus, the re-entrenchment of town planning in the face of various threatening developments signalled as a possibility in the first essay is a permanent danger, especially nowadays. Also, since that paper has been written, planning teachers have indeed organised themselves in the *Education for Planning Association* with aims including those it advocates. The next point which is unfortunately highly relevant to the situation of the late seventies is that of a glut of newly graduating planners and the employment problem which this causes. The second essay is of particular relevance to this area of great current concern. Firstly, it lays bare the reasons for this development having taken place. Secondly, it is taken out of a larger paper which is concerned with, amongst other things, the danger of just this happening. Naturally, I get little joy out of having predicted accurately what was going to happen as early as 1972!

Lastly, the "generalist-with-a-specialism" concept also appears to be of relevance nowadays. Although I do not have first-hand knowledge of developments in Britain since 1974, the impression one gets is that courses are developing in this very direction, partly as a response to the bleak employment situation. Since they diffuse the pressure on professional employment opportunities somewhat, shorter and more general undergraduate followed by professional orientated graduate courses become attractive to the planning schools. This coincides with the implementation of the Royal Town Planning Institute's latest educational policy stance described in the third essay of Part I. Therefore, we may expect the "generalist-with-a-specialism" model to have a wider appeal than hitherto. As the final essay in this volume will suggest, its relevance might be greater still. Arguably, it provides a general model for education for practice in today's world.

Planning Education:
A European View of British Experience

There are many reasons why a Continental planner might envy the achievements of his British colleagues. Planning legislation has reached a very high degree of sophistication; development control is comprehensive; the Government has been following an ambitious programme of establishing new towns which has reached a stage where the idea of creating a new community of 500,000 inhabitants in Central Lancashire has been endorsed. The institutional context of the British planners' professional activities is an incomparably more favourable one than many Continental planners dream of. Local authorities, which are mainly responsible for the implementation of planning, are of relatively larger size and better staffed. An elaborate system of ministerial control ensures that national policies are carried through at the local level, administrative performance is adequate and decisions are fair towards all parties concerned. The same ministry also provides guidelines through an increasing amount of technical literature including some remarkable statistics.

British planners in addition have reached full professional status, a fact which will concern us later. Their professional body, the Town Planning Institute, has a longstanding tradition and its membership includes several thousand planners in Britain and overseas. The professional qualification of "Chartered Town Planner" is tied to associate membership, a fact which gives the TPI considerable, if not exclusive, control over career opportunities. A shortage of qualified planners has created a sellers' market in which the average salary does not compare unfavourably with private employment.

As for planning education, the situation looks equally promising. Some 14 institutions, both universities and the second branch of the British binary system of higher education, the colleges of technology or polytechnics, offer no less than 21 courses in planning at undergraduate and postgraduate level.[1] Furthermore, the number is increasing steadily. The most outstanding tradition exists because it was Britain which pioneered the establishment of specialised study programmes for planning.

I feel that this introduction is necessary as a background to the following, sometimes rather critical remarks on the practice of British planning education. This is specially so when they are made by somebody who, coming from the Continent, has every reason to admire these achievements. But, being actively involved in the teaching of planners in one of these courses, I am experiencing some of its *prima facie* problems. An analysis of these may be of importance for other countries where planning education is at an earlier stage, and it is for this reason that I give an account of them.

The history of British planning education begins with the establishment of a postgraduate course in "Civic Design" at the University of Liverpool in 1910. This coincided with the first "Housing and Town Planning Act" and was followed by the foundation of the Town Planning Institute in 1914. It is worth noting that it was at this time that the increase in the number of so-called "Qualifying Associations" was at its peak in Britain. The accomplishments of established professional bodies, the Royal Institute of British Architects among them,[2] demonstrated the value of organisation. The evolving pattern of these professional bodies was clearly visible and included as one salient feature the introduction of examinations.[3] It is therefore not surprising that the small band of people concerned with town planning at that time followed this example and introduced an examination, the first of which was held in 1920. The architectural, engineering and surveying professions assisted in bringing these developments about and have since been the "parent professions" of town planning.

Judging from its success in the inter-war period this move towards professionalisation of planning was somewhat premature. The formation

[1]The Careers Research and Advisory Centre (CRAC), Architecture and Planning, A Guide to First Degree Courses in UK Universities, September 1967.

[2]For the development of the architectural profession see: Barrington Kaye, *The Development of the Architectural Profession in Britain*, London, 1960.

[3]Geoffrey Millerson, *The Qualifying Associations – A Study in Professionalisation*, London, 1964, pp. 183-6.

of the TPI anticipated an expanding demand which did not occur to a very substantial degree. Membership kept well under 1000 until the 1950s. Town planning was regarded as a convenient extension of their professional activities by the members of the three "parent professions". It is therefore not surprising that, although the range of activities widened somewhat with the introduction of the Town and Country Planning Summer School in 1934, the Institute did not have a full-time secretary and staff until 1946.

Even more significant, professionalisation had begun at a time when the theoretical basis of planning merely consisted of some purely ideological propositions. I suspect that the very acceptance of town planning had something to do with the promises of these propositions, promises which contained partial solutions to the problems of an emerging fully industrialised society, e.g. through the dispersion of population, etc. What has been said of the neighbourhood concept, namely that its "latent function does contribute to the stability of society . . . though its actual manifest content is highly questionable",[4] applies in all probability to the ideology of the town planning profession as a whole.

It was only after the Second World War that a turning point was reached. The atmosphere towards the end of the war was most favourable for planning in Britain. A number of royal commissions had worked out elaborate proposals for planning policy which were implemented in the "New Towns Act" of 1946 and the development of the British planning machinery which is today the object of envious admiration on the part of outsiders.

The expansion of planning after the war very quickly resulted in a shortage of qualified personnel and made the development of planning education a pressing problem. In 1949, a "Committee on the Qualifications for Planners" (Schuster Committee)[5] was set up to review the situation and to make recommendations. Up until then few conspicuous changes had taken place since the establishment of the course

---

[4]N. Dennis, The Popularity of the Neighbourhood Community Idea, *Sociological Review*, Vol. 6, Dec. 1958, pp. 191-206. For a thorough investigation of the ideological promises of planning and of the planners' professional ideology see: Heide Berndt, Das Gesellschaftsbild bei Stadtplanern, Stuttgart-Bern, 1968.

[5]*Committee on the Qualifications for Planners*, HMSO, 1950, Cmd. 8059.

at Liverpool. The two principal innovations had been the forging of a link between the TPI and the planning schools through the instrument of exemption from the Institute's examinations for graduates of approved courses and, secondly, the introduction of a five-year undergraduate course leading towards a BA Honours Degree in "Town and Country Planning".[6] Both innovations proved to have considerable impact on later developments.

The "Schuster Committee", although considering the possibility of an undergraduate education for planning, was inclined to favour postgraduate courses. The most interesting recommendations, however, were aimed at relaxing the tight grip which the "parent professions" had on the TPI and its membership. For reasons which are understandable from the point of view of professional self-interest these were never implemented.

The next fifteen years were perhaps the most turbulent in the development of the British planning profession. A severe conflict of interests raged in the Institute which in itself is a challenge for the sociology of professions to explain.[7]

The prelude to this conflict came from the architectural profession which has more than 20,000 members. The architect-planners claimed a dominant position in planning because of their training in three-dimensional design. It is difficult to say whether their subsequent demands for a quicker way of qualifying for architects were indeed a take-over bid, but it is beyond doubt that the rank-and-file members of the TPI regarded them as such. The allegations were that members of the Royal Institute of British Architects, who were at the same time leading members of the TPI had been instructed to work themselves up to the governing bodies of the Institute and to open its membership for architects. Conversely it was from the "direct-entry planners", i.e. those who had a prime allegiance to, and a prime interest in planning as a career, that resistance to these proposals came, which finally resulted not only in their rejection, but also in a remarkable shift of emphasis in the policy of the Institute.

[6]The first course of this kind was introduced at the Newcastle division of the University of Durham in 1945.

[7]In what follows I am referring to a dissertation submitted at the Faculty of Social Sciences of the University of Southampton: R. S. Dolden, *The Town Planners: A Study in Professionalisation*, 1968.

The basic change was to a "generalist" concept of the planner's professional role. What this means is clearly stated in the Revised Scheme for the Final Examination due to come into operation by 1970:

"Town Planning is a process, involving a recurring cycle of operations, for preparing and controlling the implementation of plans for changing systems of land-use and settlement of varying scale. In this activity the chartered planner plays the central and crucial professional role. His special skill, a command of the planning process as a whole, qualifies and entitles him to organise and co-ordinate all planning operations as well as to design and control the implementation of the plan or policy.

In addition to the chartered town planner, there are numerous persons in other disciplines or professions who participate in the planning process and make essential contributions to it."[8]

We may welcome this role for the planner, and indeed there is much to be said for the implications for educational policy to be drawn from it. But we should not deceive ourselves about the ideological character of this new concept, which reflects the self-interest of members of the TPI as much as a serious concern for and appreciation of the role of the planner. Furthermore, however progressive this "generalist" concept of the planner may have been, there is the possibility of it degenerating into a retrogressive one under pressure from the social sciences. There are already fears of a challenge from these disciplines which combine breadth of scope and methodological rigour. An example of this challenge is the mushrooming of organisations, research establishments and university courses which concern themselves with the same range of problems as the planning profession. Another is a recent move on the part of the government to introduce a community redevelopment programme in twelve urban areas on the lines of the American experience, in which town planners have not so far played any part. Other examples could be added, such as an advertisement for the post of a "Head of Research and Intelligence" for the City of Sheffield, with requirements which include a degree in economics or statistics but not in planning.

The challenge is there. If you allow me to speculate about the likely response of the planning profession, then let me say that I anticipate initial resistance against opening it up. There will be a reaffirmation of its high

[8]Town Planning Institute, Examination Handbook, October 1967, p. 35.

valuation of the efficiency of land-use, and there will be an increased emphasis on aesthetic values. The effect on the planning profession may be to let it develop in the direction of rather narrow, technical and aesthetic expertise with a considerable command of public-relations techniques with which to marshal support from relevant pressure groups.

However, the grave social problems which local authorities will face over the next decade or so may result in physical or land-use planning becoming a matter for a fringe department of local government, the activities of which will be of rather marginal importance to the community as a whole. It is only outside the confines of such departments that − assuming that this analysis is right − we expect a substantial broadening of the scope of planning. To make students fit for this change, to give them the capacity for learning and for grasping the essential relationships in the outside world, is the objective towards which I should like planning education to strive.

But before we turn to the future let me outline what the shift of emphasis in the ideology of the British planning profession towards a "generalist" concept of the planner's role entailed for planning education. I hope to be able to show that there is considerable logic in it.

The implications are twofold. They affect content and institutional form of planning education. Let us deal with form first:

Whereas the "Schuster Committee" had favoured postgraduate courses, it was now said that the "test of the planning profession's claim to a distinct field of activity is the practicability of framing an undergraduate educational programme".[9] Not only did the emphasis shift towards undergraduate courses, but it was stated that the exemption from the Institute's Final Examination was equivalent to a university level qualification. In consequence the Institute favoured the expansion of courses in independent departments in well-established universities, or institutions of equivalent status.

As to the content of planning education, the Institute published a new syllabus for its Final Examination.[10] Its importance lies not so much in the fact that candidates would have to follow it in their preparation,

[9]R. H. Kantorowich, Education for Planning, *Journal of the Town Planning Institute*, Vol. 53, May 1967, pp. 175-84.

[10]See Examination Handbook, *op.cit.*

because nowadays only a minority enters the profession by way of its Final Examination. It is rather that the Institute follows this syllabus as a guideline in its policy of recognising particular courses for exemption from its Final Examination. I should like you to become aware of the fact that this is an exceptionally powerful instrument which makes for a certain uniformity in the approach of planning education on part of all recognised schools throughout the country.

The TPI's revised syllabus is a rather complicated one, and it would take us too long to go into the details. Let me only say very briefly that it seems somewhat ambiguous to me, insofar as it recognises on the one hand the existence of specialisms in planning which are related to the different levels on which physical planning is being undertaken, but on the other hand still requires candidates to have a well-rounded knowledge in all of them. Believe me, the syllabus has been very carefully designed for this end.

Again I leave it completely open whether these implications are in themselves a good thing or not. They clearly mirror the new role-concept of the "generalist" planner by attempting to ensure a minimum common base, and they complement the planning profession's need for recognition as a respectable profession in its own right. By the way, before I forget to mention it, there is consensus about this new syllabus being much better than the old one.

The scene is set for an appreciation of the circumstances under which undergraduate courses operated. It is mainly in this field where I have gathered some limited experience, and this is the type of course which you may be mostly interested in. I wish to stress, however, that my observations are of what I believe to be a fairly general nature, applying in all probability to most courses of the same kind, if not always to the same degree.

Another point before I start: you may, coming from a different context where planning education has not yet advanced to a stage where undergraduate courses are regarded as being feasible, feel that it is pointless to criticise something which undoubtedly you want to achieve in your sphere. Let me state, therefore, that I am committed to the idea of undergraduate planning courses, but that I want to point out to you that they generate considerable difficulties unless the theory behind them is unambiguous.

Let us deal with the favourable circumstances first:

(1) The British planning environment is one in which awareness of planning is very widespread. One occasion which springs to mind is that of a young hitch-hiker, solidly working class, who, when I mentioned that I was lecturing in planning, had some not too friendly comments about planning. Mind you, he came from the ill-famed housing estates of Portsmouth. Another, perhaps more favourable piece of evidence for the public awareness of planning is the existence of numerous middle-class associations up and down the country, which concern themselves with the quality of the physical environment. Their cooperation has been institutionalised through the public participation provisions of the "Town and Country Planning Act" of 1968.

(2) Planning education takes place in the institutional context of a rapidly expanding system of higher education with its many innovations, which in itself would be the subject of many talks.

(3) I feel very strongly that it is an advantage to have a student-body which is in part at least highly committed to planning as a career.

(4) The great amount of expertise brought together in planning schools is quite extraordinary by Continental standards.

There are, of course, also constraints. I want to deal with them in somewhat more detail:

(1) The concept of a planner, although clearly defined, is, as I have taken pains to explain, an ideological one. There is continuing questioning of this concept, especially since there are as yet very few qualified planners who have gone through an undergraduate planning course themselves.

(2) We maintain that planning is a profession in its own right, educating people to be exclusively planners. However, one of the main elements in the concept of professionalism is a skill based on theory. We have to accept that planning theory is still rather underdeveloped.

(3) The concept of the planner on the other hand inhibits us from relying more significantly on other academic disciplines which may help us out of the dilemma of not having a sound theory.

In accordance with the TPI's definition of the role of a contributor to the planning process one is sometimes compelled to treat other sciences as auxiliary forces, ruling out the possibility that they could have something to say about the very process of planning itself. This means that we have a cluster of theoretically sophisticated disciplines around a somewhat nebulous core termed planning. One is reminded of Britton Harris, who said once: "We have a great need for a science of planning in order to establish what is the role of science in planning."[11]

(4) Not only are the courses geared towards the syllabus of the Institute's Final Examination, but they are also compelled to teach every student practically everything included there. The desire to structure courses leads only too easily to the idea of a certain hierarchical order, starting with local planning, village planning, urban planning, subregional and regional planning, national planning, etc. What is implied is that the problems on the different levels have an increasing complexity and thus should be tackled in some order. One of the implications is that the first part of a course emphasises physical design, whereas the final part is somewhat more abstract, which may be frustrating to some students.

(5) As a result students are taken through a fairly rigid course in which very little choice is left to them. Given a particular theory about what human beings are and want, it is therefore not surprising that the limited amount of self-direction results in the students' involvement with the course sometimes leaving something to desire. I don't want to take this any further, except to point out to you that some new thinking about the conditions under which innovative behaviour can be expected in education is going on at some places. I think for instance that the "Middle-School" experiment of the Architectural Association School deserves our attention. Here they have managed to

[11]Britton Harris, The Limits of Science and Humanism in Planning, *Journal of the American Institute of Planners*, Vol. 33, September 1967, pp. 324-35.

involve the students in setting their own problems.[12]

(6) There is, of course, the danger implied in any "generalist" concept of it degenerating into superficiality. In addition, although the TPI maintains that all recognised courses are of the same level as a first degree in a university, some of them lead to a diploma only. These students, in the majority, may have less chance to go for a further degree in order to acquire specialist knowledge. Such are the intricacies of the British system of higher education where diplomas do not in general qualify for postgraduate courses. It is therefore possible that a high proportion of diploma-holders will remain without any substantial sort of specialism, which may be to their disadvantage.

(7) For understandable reasons planning courses are geared towards providing qualified manpower for turning the wheels of the fairly elaborate British planning machinery. But there is of course the distinctive possibility of substantial changes in the planning machinery itself during the professional careers of present-day students[13] until well after 2000. The problem is, of course, how to teach them their skills in a way which will make them transferable to other problem areas.

(8) A further point is the attitude towards research. It seems to me as if there was a strong emphasis on professional training and a concomitant neglect of academic ideals in planning education. In particular there may not be enough weight given to the advancement of knowledge as against the mere transmission of existing practices. It may be possible to relate this to the failure of planners in planning research. Because it must not go unnoticed that apparently only a minor proportion of research in our field is undertaken by planners, although I admit that this

[12]See: John Lloyd, Education for choice and change, and Anthony Wade, The middle school experiment, both in "Arena", *Architectural Association Journal*, Vol. 84, No. 923, June–July 1968.

[13]Consider only the changes which would result from a reorganisation of local government. It is commonly assumed that the Royal Commission on Local Government, which is expected to report soon, will come up with some drastic proposals for the reduction in the number of authorities.

can be attributed in parts at least to the difference in sheer manpower between planning and other disciplines.

In what follows in practical proposals I build partly on the ideas of Harvey S. Perloff, whose classic in the field of planning education was published a dozen years ago and, to the best of my knowledge, has never been matched since. Unfortunately it has never been made the basis of another course — again according to my knowledge — since the Chicago experiment, on which Perloff's book was based, ended in 1956.[14]

The assumptions on which my proposals are based are the following:
  (1) That there is a common element to all planning activities.
  (2) That this common element consists of a core of theoretical disciplines of very wide applicability.
  (3) That it is the duty of academics to take on the task of developing this core and thus taking the lead — as indeed they did in many other disciplines.
  (4) That the planning schools are in a position to develop this core although a substantial part of it will be drawn from other disciplines.

The last assumption may be the most doubtful one, particularly since the development of such fields as operations research, systems analysis and cybernetics, which have each taken such a dynamic character. But I would maintain that there is still a fair chance for planning to take up this challenge successfully. The implications for structure and content of planning courses can be summed up under four headings: "general education", "planning core", "generalist-with-a-specialism", "problem-oriented project work".

(1) General Education

The argument about "general" or "liberal" education as an element of higher education is widespread. Admittedly, the importance attached to this element must vary from one institutional setting to another. I am therefore not necessarily arguing for the introduction of music, drama, and

[14]Harvey S. Perloff, *Education for Planning — City, State and Regional*, Baltimore, 1957.

medieval literature as formal parts of the curriculum. It is only that I should like to see some liberal elements being introduced as objectives of teaching in all subjects connected with the course. These would include the ability to communicate verbally and in writing, and some orientation to the outside world, both of which I think are of paramount importance. This may sound rather mundane, but believe me, it is one of the difficulties we are up against. We must meet this difficulty without really spelling out that it is existent, which means that we cannot devote enough time and energy to it.

I hope to have demonstrated how the constraints of the environment of planning education mould undergraduate courses. You may have noticed that I referred neither to individual performance nor to particular weaknesses of our School. Indeed, I would expect to find these problems in roughly the same form in all establishments, even in those with a much longer tradition than our relatively new School has. The essence of an analysis of the kind I have attempted is, plainly, that it is independent from individual performance.

You may find that the situation looks grim and that there is nothing one can do about it. This would be to take a far too deterministic viewpoint. Innovation in the institutional context itself could alter the situation substantially.

Admittedly, for those reasons which I outlined above, the TPI is unlikely to become a source of innovation. The Institute is just in the process of bringing its Revised Examination Syllabus into operation. Its education committee furthermore is busy with approving or rejecting courses up and down the country, so that on face value it has every justification to look with complacency into a consolidated future.

It is rather from the planning schools themselves that I expect some sort of initiative in the direction of a more general form of education to arise in the future. Thus far it was the TPI which held a tight grip on each individual school through the instrument of its recognition. But with the conspicuous growth of planning schools both in numbers and in importance, with the continuous increase in their manpower, they are bound to make their weight felt. Frankly, what I want to see is some institutional framework in which planning educationalists can propagate and defend their interests against the Town Planning Institute. This could take the form of a consultative committee of the planning schools. More likely, an association of teachers in planning education might perform this role.

Why do I expect this development to take place? Indeed, why do I call for conflict between the TPI and the planning schools? It is because I believe that the latter may become concerned about being subject to visitations by TPI boards which may not even comprise a single educationalist. It is because I think that awareness is increasing that education has problems in its own right, and that the planning schools' concern for the future of their students may soon override their desire to serve the immediate ends of the practitioners. It is also because I think that academic institutions have broader obligations than simply those to the profession. For instance, they should take their measure from the values and norms of the academic world itself. It is precisely from the academic world that pressure may be generated to improve the academic standing of planning courses.

(2) Planning Core

This is clearly the most critical part of this proposal on which the whole argument hinges. Nevertheless I do not feel sufficiently competent to specify its content very clearly. Let us perhaps establish only that there must be this planning-core; that the concentrated efforts of planning educationalists should be directed towards determining its structure and content; and that it should have as wide an applicability as possible. By implication this would mean that it would focus on the way in which decisions are arrived at and implemented by different agents rather than on the substance of these decisions. This would certainly mean a heavy reliance on social and political theory which I personally would welcome anyway. It would equally mean probing into philosophy.

The "general education" element and the "planning core" should enable the student to apply theoretical concepts skilfully to all processes concerned with deliberate change, and to see their common element. This should be a skill applicable in different present and future contexts. I would therefore stress the value of such an element in planning education with particular reference to the likely changes during a professional career.

(3) Generalist-with-a-Specialism

If specialism develops on the basis of fairly general appreciation of the theoretical core, then there is certainly no harm in it. Indeed, it would be foolish to deny the great virtues of specialist knowledge. It is really only the narrow-mindedness of specialism which we oppose.

It is hard to conceive of a complete list of all specialisms which could be included. They cover the whole range from physical design to social and economic policy. It is therefore probably inconceivable to teach them all in one institution. I would rather like to see institutions specialising, which would however probably mean adopting a two-tier degree structure, with a first degree awarded for completion of the core-programme of roughly comparable standard, structure, and content in many institutions, and a second degree awarded for the specialism, which could then be taken at quite a different institution. This is a fairly familiar pattern in the Anglo-Saxon world and there is really no reason why it should not be adopted in planning education as well.

(4) Problem-oriented Project Work

Studio work is one of the holy cows of planning education. Indeed, the relaxed atmosphere of untidy studios, where students and teachers spend many evenings sipping coffee, having most informal contacts and doing an excessive amount of sheer physical work, is one of the most cherished parts of the culture of planning schools. Unfortunately I am not exactly convinced that all this is very conducive towards the development of the attitudes and values which I would like a planner to adopt. It is for this reason that I argue very strongly for rethinking the whole rationale of project work.

One can distinguish three objectives of project work.

(a) PROBLEM-ORIENTATION

Any project should deal with a problem which is of true concern to somebody in the outside world. This is frankly not always the case with projects, especially when fairly vague aesthetic ideals are made the basis of work set.

Problems can be most diverse in nature. Analysis of problems must form an important part of projects, which may sometimes involve pieces of genuine research. It can be assumed that the intellectual capacity of analysing a problem, once acquired, can be applied to other problems as well. Therefore, it seems unnecessary to assume that a certain sequence or a certain hierarchy of problems must be investigated.

(b) ACTION-ORIENTATION

Projects must come up with proposals for action based on analysis, evaluation and choice. Choices are under many constraints in the outside world which it is difficult to appreciate from the drawing board. Role-playing, gaming, and simulation may overcome some of these difficulties. But perhaps there is another device which is far too neglected, and this is the case study. It is perhaps worth noting that even the teaching of engineering design has reverted to case studies of particular design problems, which are said to be more revealing than half-hearted simulations of real-life situations.[15] There are enough examples of good case studies in the American literature especially.[16] I believe that this method is an adequate one for increasing the appreciation of planning problems, and that it leaves enough scope for creativity through the possibility of putting forward alternative proposals.

(c) INNOVATIVE BEHAVIOUR

This brings us to the last desired objective of project-work — to instill innovative behaviour. The concept may not be entirely clear, but it seems to depend to a very large extent on the degree to which the individual is

[15]H. O. Fuchs, *The Function of Case Histories in Teaching Engineering Design*, Institution of Engineering Design, Conference Proceedings, Part 1, July 1966, pp. 24-8.

[16]The one which springs immediately to one's mind is the classic by M. Meyerson and E. C. Banfield, *Politics, Planning and the Public Interest — The Case of Public Housing in Chicago*, Glencoe (Ill.), 1955.

actively involved. Whereas there is no doubt about the value of group work, it can be organised in many different manners, and the individual can be related to the group structure in varying ways. The literature provides some useful material which is directly relevant to this problem.[17]

What can be said with a fair amount of confidence is that preconceived, rigidly defined programmes which ask for one kind of solution only, and which are handed out to the whole year indiscriminately at the same time, criticised at a set date, and marked according to a fixed scale, are not exactly the kinds of projects which encourage innovative behaviour. What is rather asked for is a plurality of approaches to a multitude of problems, involving students in different forms of cooperation, and in the definition of their situation both in terms of the problem they set for themselves, and in terms of their approaches towards it. Then I would expect the library desk to become as important in project work as the drawing board, the typewriter as omnipresent as the T-square, the questionnaire as maps, the interview as the appraisal of visual qualities, in short, the brains as important as the all too often very personal feeling about right and wrong which seems to occupy such a central place in project work today.

In summary, and assuming there is some validity to the idea of a common element in all planning activities, planning education must develop around a core. It must, furthermore, give the students the ability to communicate, to orient themselves, and to acquire learning techniques. It must instill in them the desire of doing something about problems, and it should give them detailed knowledge about one area of specialisation, which could of course be physical design. But it must not stick to the narrow idea of producing physical planners only.

---

[17]For example, one could deduce from a study commissioned by the Royal Institute of British Architects and published under the title *The Architect and his Office* (London 1962) that the degree to which the individual is involved through discussions and mutual criticism increases his satisfaction.

The "Specialist" versus "Generalist" Conflict 1963-5

This essay describes an episode in the history of the British town planning profession during the sixties which has come to be known as the "specialist" versus "generalist" conflict. During this conflict, the planning profession re-cast its self-image from that of a profession consisting mainly of people with a basic qualification in another profession into one of a profession in its own right. This signifies a stage of the process of professionalisation — that of subjective recognition of the existence of a distinct body of expertise.

The interpretation of this conflict offered in this essay rests on the following four points:

(1) The partial implementation of the Schuster Committee's proposals of the fifties for widening the basis of membership of the TPI had effectively created *two classes of members* with differences in power (through control over the Council) and status (younger Corporate Members of the Institute were Associate Members until, at a later stage of their career, they became Members). One class was that of double-qualified architect-planners, engineer-planners or surveyor-planners who had the backing of their respective professional institutes; the other class consisted of "direct-entry" planners (either by way of the Intermediate and Final Examination of the Institute or — increasingly — by way of undergraduate courses) *and* graduates from academic disciplines who had qualified through postgraduate courses. I shall describe these as "planners only", thus signifying their prime interest in planning as their only profession.

(2) The rift between these two classes widened because many "planners only" saw their *way to the top blocked by double-qualified chief officers* and because local authorities *continued to prefer technically qualified chief planning officers*, that is architect-planners, engineer-planners, etc.

(3) As a consequence of this situation the "planners only" reacted to a challenge from the Royal Institute of British Architects (RIBA) by

27

overthrowing a Council inclined towards the "specialist" position and by attempting to *carve out their own technical "specialism" for the handling of the planning process.*

(4) The conflict concerned planning as a bureaucratic function, not as a philosophical and/or reformist idea. Both "generalists" and "specialists" staked a claim for the *physical planning function in local government*. "Comprehensive" planning, either in the sense of Schuster's "positive planning", or in the current sense of local authority policies planning, was not at issue.

The Parties Concerned

Although based to a certain degree on conjecture rather than on evidence (not all facts are available) these observations seem to amount to the most meaningful interpretation of available data. This interpretation requires redefining the basic division between "generalists" and "specialists". During the debate, it has often been suggested that a "generalist" was somebody who has qualified in planning by way of an undergraduate planning course or by the Institute's own Intermediate and Final Examinations, and a "specialist" somebody with no matter what first degree and a planning qualification. Much as the Schuster Committee had done before, this distinction neglected the fundamental distinction between a graduate in any of the social sciences qualified in planning ("geographer-planner", "economist-planner", "sociologist-planner") and a member of the TPI who was, at the same time, member of any of the parent professions ("architect-planner", "engineer-planner", "surveyor-planner"). As a matter of fact, the "generalist" position, although saying that planning was a profession in its own right and that it was thus feasible to qualify in planning only, was nevertheless held by most of those members who were graduates in one of the social sciences and who had afterwards qualified in planning, as well as by the "direct-entry" planners. These two groups had a prime allegiance to planning as a profession, and I shall call them *"planners only"*. The "specialist" position was predominantly held by double-qualified members with their consequent double-allegiance and not by all members who, according to the original definition were *also* specialists. The definition of a "specialist" as advanced by the proponents of the "specialist" line therefore did not reflect the true divisions within the membership of the TPI. On the contrary, whether by conscious design or not, it had as its latent purpose to divide the ranks of those whom I have called "planners only", and thus to perpetuate the grip which the "parent professions" had on the TPI. To the extent that this was true, the definition of a specialist was ideological. To paraphrase George Orwell in *Animal Farm*: Some were more specialist than others!

Prelude

The conflict itself was preceded by a move on the part of the Royal Institute of British Architects (RIBA) early in 1956. The background to this move was a sharp decline in confidence in planning during the fifties, accompanied by a partial dismantling of the planning machinery under a Conservative government. In a report approved by the Council of the RIBA the following factors were held responsible for this:

(a) Failure of the planning machine to justify planning controls with view to creative work done;

(b) Reduction of the role played by the Ministry of Housing and Local Government;

(c) Delegation of powers from the counties to urban districts;

(d) Dispersion of powers to a number of ministries (i.e. Board of Trade, Ministry of Transport, etc.).[1]

In a policy statement, the RIBA then suggested *strengthening the role of the architect in planning* by demanding that certain planning posts be held for architects only. The statement read:

"(A) That all County Boroughs should employ an Architect as a Chief Officer and that he should also be responsible for Town Planning.

(B) That all large Boroughs and Urban Districts should employ an Architect with local planning duties depending on the degree of delegation.

(C) That in cases where County Planning Officers are not Architects, County Architects should advise Planning Committees on development control in small towns, and in rural districts and

[1]Notes from the Minutes of the Council, *Royal Institute of British Architects Journal*, Vol. 63, (1956), No. 8, p. 362.

villages, and should be adequately staffed to enable them to deal with broad problems of landscape as well as building."[2]

Why was it that the *architects* made this move? There are a number of reasons. First of all, the implementation of the Schuster Committee's proposals had had the effect of *reducing the proportion of "specialist" entrants to the profession*, in the case of the architects not so much by reducing the number of architect-entrants but rather by swelling the ranks of "direct-entry" planners and holders of degrees other than architecture, engineering and surveying.

Not only did the architect-planners decline as a proportion of the membership of the TPI, but so did, of course, the engineer-planners and surveyor-planners, although their loss was less significant simply because their position had been less dominant from the outset. It may be, however, that the sensitivity of the architects to the loss of their hold on planning was greater also because with *their professional area of concern being less specific* and less well-defined than that of the other "specialist", they enjoyed less *job-security*. Otherwise it would be difficult to understand why the architects should have pressed the case of the "specialists" so much harder than the other professions, and why they should have reacted more strongly than anybody else to the TPI opting for the "generalist" line after 1965.

The "Lane Report" and Reactions from Branches

Within the TPI the overture to the conflict came in the Presidential Addresses of 1961 and 1962, which led to the establishment of the "Special Committee of Recruitment and Membership (Lane Committee)", which reported to the Branches in May, 1963.

The report stressed the decline of "specialist" entries to the profession from 50% (1954-7) to 36% (1958-61) and concluded that there was an ". . . urgent need to review . . . present methods of recruitment to see what can be done to encourage more architects, surveyors and engineers to qualify as Town Planners."[3]

[2] *op. cit.*

[3] The Town Planning Institute, *Recruitment and Membership Report of a Special Committee under the Chairmanship of Mr. L. W. Lane*, 1963.

The reasons given were an actual and anticipated shortage of planning staff based on the "Membership Survey" conducted in 1962. The fundamental proposition was: "... that the profession should embrace within its corporate membership both generalists and specialists all of whom will be trained to be members of the planning team."[4]

To achieve this end, the "final Examination should be revised to provide for many within these professions who will wish their contribution to planning to make the fullest possible use of the special skill which they acquired rather than that they should be examined in fields of planning with which they may not ultimately be ... concerned."[5]

The resulting proposals for the Final Examination were such as to give all candidates an understanding of the basic principles and practice of planning and to allow them to take an advanced test in their specialism. This was accompanied amongst others by proposals for introducing other-than-corporate classes of membership, and for accepting work done in a specialist capacity as qualifying practical experience. On top of this, direct membership could be extended "... to cover persons 45 years of age (instead of 50 as it was until then — A.F.) who, although not qualified in the profession, have nevertheless made a substantial contribution to planning but at this stage of their career cannot be expected to sit the Institute's examinations...."[6]

There was also a statement on the Institute's staffing situation, the fact that it had to look for new premises and on its financial situation in general. One strong incentive on the part of the TPI for widening the membership of the Institute may thus have been the desire to secure adequate financing for its activities.

As Millerson suggests, a small number of practitioners has in many cases been a special obstacle to professionalisation.[7] As a general rule, inadequate finance has *always* implied the *danger of widening the*

[4]*op. cit.*

[5]*op. cit.*

[6]*op. cit.*

[7]G. Millerson, *The Qualifying Associations – A Study in Professionalisation*, London, 1964, p. 186.

association's appeal to attract those from bordering specialities. Also to *offer concessions to experienced people* to encourage them to join follows a fairly general pattern in a situation of financial strain. This puts the move by the TPI's Council into perspective — despite the emphatic denial of a link between the membership-issue and financial considerations which was issued afterwards to reverse the impression created by the Lane Report.

Another point which must have loomed large in the minds of Council Members advocating opening the profession was that of the then anticipated rise of central area development and traffic schemes in the wake of the Buchanan Report. Naturally, the expectation was that of a need for additional architects and highway engineers thus giving the Council reasons to press for assimilating more of these into the profession. This expectation was not borne out by subsequent developments during which structure and subregional planning became the pacemakers.

The reactions of the Branches were near to unanimous in their disapproval. The growth of the Institute was considered to be healthy by the rank-and-file of the membership, and the need for widening its intake was not accepted. In particular, the issue of attracting more professionals was seen to be coupled with finance (see above). On the whole, the underlying intention of *all* the recommendations was seen as that of making things easier for other professionals to enter planning and thereby helping to solve the Institute's financial problems. Hence, the Secretary reported: "There seems to be a sense of grievance that the interests of the man who has taken up planning as a profession in its own right and has no other professional qualification have been largely overlooked by the Special Committee."[8]

He also drew attention to a "strong body of adverse criticism against the proposals which are considered to be 'diluting' the overall standard of entry to the profession in order to attract a particular type of planner."[9]

The reactions of the Branches validate the points made earlier about the results of the Schuster Committee's proposals. There was, for instance, strong animosity between *"planners only"* and *"specialists"*, i.e. double-qualified planners: "Town planning should be the *basic* skill and

[8]The Town Planning Institute, *Summary of Views of Branches and Individual Members* (mimeo).

[9]*op. cit.*

specialisation should follow" (South West of England Branch).

"Majority thought it was ... unrealistic to expect other professions to provide most of future planners, if so planning would continue to be looked on as a secondary profession ..." (North of England Division, Northern Group).

"The Report concentrates on 'specialists' and does not sufficiently consider the interest of the man who is trained only as a planner and whose whole career is in planning" (individual comment).

"Town planning is not a simple *extension* of architecture and surveying" (individual comment).[10]

In some comments this adverse feeling was explicitly linked to chances for promotion to chief planning officer: "TPI should press for termination of the 'dual-qualification' requirement of many authorities when advertising generalist posts" (individual comment).[11]

For the same reason, support was also expressed for the TPI "Circular on Separate Planning Departments" which had been sent to local authorities earlier on.[12] It was finally noticeable that the reaction of the rank-and-file was to press for recognition of town planning as a *profession in its own right*: "To accept specialists as such into the planning team would conflict with the image of planning as a profession in its own right" (South East of England Branch).

"Proposals might well *wipe out Town Planning as separate Profession*" (individual comment).

"Role of the Town Planning Institute is to protect the interest of *planning as profession* ..." (individual comment).[13]

Despite these comments the Council referred the Report back to the "Special Committee" for further consideration.

[10]*op. cit.*

[11]*op. cit.*

[12]The Town Planning Institute, Planning Administration — The Establishment of Separate Planning Departments, A Statement of Policy by The Town Planning Institute, *Journal of the Town Planning Institute*, Vol. 49, March 1963, p. 76.

[13]*Summary of Views, op. cit.* (italics mine).

The Membership Survey and the Goss Report

A great deal of the discussion turned on the future need for planners. Indeed, both sides based their arguments on the anticipation of a great deficit in qualified planners: The "specialists" had introduced this point into the discussion, based on their post-Buchanan Report expectations referred to above and the "generalists", after having won the Council over to their point of view, pressed it too.

The earliest figure quoted is one given by Professor J. James at the Institute's Educational Conference in 1964. He estimated the number of additional chartered town planners needed to amount to 5000 over the next few years.[14] The earliest official figures about the planning profession's anticipations of future expansion are those submitted to the Mallaby Committee.

"In their written evidence the Institute stated that it had been estimated that a further 3000–4000 qualified planners would be needed to meet requirements over the immediate years ahead".[15]

The Institute's view of a shortage of qualified planners was apparently endorsed by the Mallaby Report which ascribed it to the "rapid expansion of planning work and of the demand for planners which has outstripped the resources of the planning schools".[16]

Presumably, all these figures rested on a survey of the employment of planners conducted in 1962. Though never published, a great deal of its findings became known through the Goss Report.[17] As far as one can see from this source, the approach taken to calculating this figure was one which was very familiar to planners used to establishing professional standards, i.e. input measures. The survey calculated ratios of planning staff to population in different authorities, and also of qualified staff to unqualified staff. It then postulated that those ratios found in high-status authorities should become standard. This did not involve the consideration of *actual* demand and was thus only a reflection of the planning

[14]Quoted after J. C. Holliday and G. A. G. Miller, *Planning Educational Resources for Town Planning* (mimeo).

[15]HMSO, *Committee on Staffing of Local Government*, London 1967, para. 90.

[16]*op. cit.*, para. 94.

[17]A. Goss, *The Architect and Town Planning – A Report Presented to the Council of the RIBA*, London 1965.

profession's own desire for the expansion of planning departments and the appointment of "qualified" staff.

This element of self-assurance in the "Membership Survey" of 1962 throws light on subsequent developments. The educational policy of the TPI has been based on the findings of the "Membership Survey" ever since. But the basis for the anticipated demand for additional planners was nothing but the profession's own view on what this demand ought to be! This view provided the rationale for the ensuing rapid expansion of planning education. If it happens that there is an overproduction of qualified town planners in the seventies then it is here that one would have to look for one of its root-causes.

At the time when the Council of the TPI discussed the Lane Report, the Royal Institute of British Architects commissioned Anthony Goss to compile a report on "The Architect and Town Planning". There has constantly been considerable ill-feeling amongst the rank-and-file membership about double-allegiance of members of the Council of the TPI. It may therefore be as well to check on the persons involved as members of the Steering Committee of that Report. They were: Arthur Ling, as Chairman, Council-member of the TPI, who as its President in 1968/9, i.e. long *after* the conflict had been resolved, would again argue the case of the specialist in planning; Walter Bor, Colin Buchanan, Council member and President of the TPI in 1963/4, under whose presidency it was decided to continue the efforts to widen the membership basis of the TPI by including the contributors to the planning process; Gordon Graham and A. Douglas Jones, both non-members of the TPI, and Leslie Lane, Chairman of the "Special Committee on Recruitment and Membership" and President in 1964/5, as a nominee of the TPI (who withdrew at the stage when recommendations for Royal Institute policy were formulated). Anthony Goss himself was also a Council member of the TPI. The allegations of interference from the RIBA, and of active support for these efforts from the establishment of the TPI, which were frequently made by the rank-and-file membership were thus not wholly unfounded, at least as far as the membership of this "Steering Committee" was concerned: *Four out of seven people involved were Council-members of the TPI including the two Presidents in the decisive years 1963/4 and 1964/5.*

The Goss Report itself is the most comprehensive published work on the employment of planners and their qualifications. Goss used the findings of surveys conducted into the employment of architect-planners, as well as the TPI's "Membership Survey" of 1962, though with different results as regards the number of additional qualified planners needed (1000). In the conclusions to this report, the author argued the case of the "specialist" in planning, with the main emphasis on the architect's skill on the local level, in town design. On the basis of this report the Steering Committee defined the roles of the architect in planning as follows:

(a) Design of buildings and groups of buildings;

(b) Direct engagement in the planning process:

"Architects have a contribution to make on all levels of planning", but especially on the local level: ". . . where town design and redevelopment should form a large sector of the work, the design skill of the architect must play a decisive part. . . . Architecture is the only profession which trains people for the design of the built environment . . . (Therefore) the architectural profession has an *inalienable interest in planning. . . .* It is *inconceivable that the RIBA could . . . accept the idea that planning is such a distinct and separate professional activity that architects have no part to play unless* they qualify in a separate profession.

Though architectural skill *must play a leading part* in local planning, other disciplines must contribute. The last few years have made it clear that major planning assignments can only be discharged by teams of persons possessing a variety of professional skills".[18]

As a consequence, the town planning content of architecture courses should be improved so as to justify shorter full-time postgraduate courses than normal for exemption from the Final Examination of the TPI. The Committee pointed out that, under the existing system of training, it could require as long as eleven years to qualify in architecture and planning. Besides, they complained: "It is much easier for *geographers*, who have completed a three-years undergraduate course, to obtain grants for a two-year postgraduate course in planning than it is for an architect who has completed a five-year course".[19]

This all should help to restore to planning its ". . . essential design

[18]*op. cit.*, p. 69.

[19]*op. cit.*, p. 70.

content" and to "mobilise, and persuade planning authorities to use, *all existing resources of architects and architect/planners*".[20]

This they deemed to be even more important since the ". . . use of commercial organisations by local authorities to design redevelopment schemes" resulted in "a great deal of redevelopment . . . in which neither architects nor planners, nor indeed the nation, can take pride".[21]

This, together with the recommendation of refresher courses for those "who have left planning", gives support to the view that the architectural profession's motivation to move into planning was – and perhaps still is – based on a threat to its own economic base. Thus, the TPI was faced with a situation where a powerful professional association was operating close to its own area of concern, with this association itself being hard-pressed for its economic livelihood. This is one of the hard facts of life behind the "generalist" versus "specialist" conflict.

The Council Statement of October 1964 and the Extraordinary General Meeting of January 1965

While the Goss Report was still being considered by its Steering Committee, the Council of the TPI adopted a Resolution on 29th October 1964, in which they re-affirmed their intention of introducing changes along "specialist" lines. The Resolution consisted of three points:

    (1) "That the policy for corporate membership shall extend, on the passing of suitable tests and proof of practical experience, the privilege of membership to all persons making a professional contribution to planning of a *general or specialist kind*.

    (2) That, as a matter of urgency, the examination requirements of the Institute be revised to make them appropriate to the new membership policy so as to *provide for those* who *wish to qualify over the whole field of planning and for those who wish to specialise in some part of it*; this revision to include

        (a) papers to be taken by all candidates designed to test their

[20]*op. cit.*, p. 71.

[21]*op. cit.*

knowledge of the aims and methods of planning, and (b) either papers covering a range of subjects related to planning or, in the case of candidates with an approved degree or professional qualification, the opportunity to take papers designed to test the application of their discipline to planning.

(3) That for a period of two years only the Council may admit to corporate membership persons of 40 years of age or over who are qualified in a related discipline, and are known to be contributing substantially to planning, subject to a professional interview and such test as the Council may require".[22]

This latter part of the resolution must have appeared particularly provocative in view of the fact that the earlier set of proposals, which had received such a frosty welcome from the Branches, had contained a similar proposal, but only for persons of 45 years of age or over.

In a memorandum accompanying the Resolution in which members were asked to vote on these policies, the Council explicitly turned against two criticisms which had been made by the Branches in their comments. One was that the interests of the rank-and-file membership with a qualification in "planning only" had been neglected; the other that the proposals were likely to erode the idea of planning as a distinctive professional activity. From the Council's reply it becomes very obvious that they advocated the "specialist" line: "Will the proposals be unfair to present members?" "The first responsibility of the Council is to see that the membership policy of the Institute is appropriate to the needs of planning. . . . A larger and more influential profession, more widely representative of the different interests engaged in planning cannot be otherwise than in the interests of all members, both those already in the Institute and *those to come*. The Council ask all members to keep this consideration firmly in mind."

"The idea that planning is an entirely clear-cut activity has *in the Council's view become untenable*. . . . To claim under these circumstances that town planning is the exclusive concern of members of the Institute as at present constituted, is bound to lead in the end to *other Institutes*

---

[22] The Town Planning Institute, *Membership Policy – A Memorandum by the Council to all Corporate Members*, 1964.

introducing their own planning sections and diplomas. . .".[23]

Well before the closing date for returning the voting papers (31st January 1965) 29 corporate members with Dr. Thomas Sharp as their spokesman requested an Extraordinary General Meeting which took place on 29th January 1965. For constitutional reasons this Meeting was unable to pass binding resolutions. Despite this, it was the turning point in this conflict because it made clear that the membership was strongly opposed to the Council's proposals and not prepared to see them forced through.

What the dissenting group asked for was that the voting papers be destroyed and the pursuit of the policy of extending membership to the "contributors" of the planning process discontinued. Out of the long and very heated debate which, on the request of the dissenters, was published in its full extent in a special supplement to the Journal of the TPI,[24] only those paragraphs are quoted which relate to the specific points made earlier: that the "planners only" felt their interests neglected, and as a reaction to this challenge arrived at a very definite idea about planning as a profession in its own right. What also becomes evident from these comments is that the challenge was seen to come from the architects.

"The basic argument advanced by the Council, and by *those largely unseen forces* that have been undermining the profession . . . , is that various . . . people contribute . . . to the process of town and country planning. . . .

"But let us take by way of example the profession which is mostly concerned in the take-over bid in which our Council is proposing to sell us out . . . *architecture*" (pointing out that architecture in particular overlaps with many other professions). "And this is the body that seeks to penetrate into another profession by arguments about team work. . . . (The Council has) become *the instrument of our destruction* (and has) forfeited all right to our confidence if it pursues this matter further" (Thomas Sharp).

The "bona fides of Council not in doubt (*although I do not think the first allegiance of all members is to the Institute*)" (Lewis Keeble).

Reference was made to "*pressure from other Institutions* to get their

[23]*op. cit.*

[24]The Town Planning Institute, Special Supplement on Membership Policy, *Journal of the Town Planning Institute*, Vol. 51, March 1965.

feet firmly into the field of planning education" (J. J. Brooks).

"The Education Committee is of course a dangerous radical body with several teachers on it . . . (It) was *never asked to advise on this matter. . .*" (Lewis Keeble).

"The Council's statement that planning is not 'an entirely clear-cut activity' certainly puzzles me as it has many other people. *The central core*, and not the edges, *identify professional activity. . . .*" (D. G. Robinson)[25]

The Meeting ended with a strong majority for discontinuing the proposed policy and destroying the ballot papers, an expression of intent which was, however, not binding on the Council. So the latter proceeded with counting the votes, and the following results were obtained with regard to the three items of the Resolution quoted above:[26]

	For	Against	Abstention
1.	784	914	20
2.	880	812	24
3.	532	1158	16

The total of votes cast was 1718.

Interpretation

It is, by the nature of a secret vote, obviously impossible to demonstrate directly that this was really the result of a revolt of the "planners only". This interpretation is therefore based on conjecture. It is furthermore an interpretation only of the aggregate results of this ballot. The motives of individual actors in this plot, and in particular of the group of dedicated advocates of the "generalist" line may have been much more complex. In particular, ideas concerning new developments and techniques in planning and desirable forms of planning education may have loomed large in their minds. These ideas are not necessarily reflections of the background of a person in terms of "planners only" versus "specialist". Leading advocates of the "generalist" line were, indeed, "specialists" from

[25]*op. cit.* (italics mine).

[26]*op. cit.*

the point of view of their formal qualifications.

In interpreting the aggregate results of the ballot, the first step is to look at the membership and the way it was split between "specialists" and "planners only". The closest date for which an analysis of the corporate membership exists is October 1965:[27]

	Associates	Members	Total	Group as % of Total
Direct entry planners	780	84	864	25.4
Architects	1098	189	1287	37.7
Surveyors	334	128	462	13.5
Other degrees (geographers, economists, sociologists, etc.)	419	48	467	13.7
	(error of 0.25% in total)		3404	99.7

The "paper-form" of the "specialists" should have given them a majority of 60:40. If the hypothesis of the "planners only" ("direct entry planners" + "other degrees") revolting against the "specialists" should hold true, then the only reasonable explanation is that a smaller proportion of "specialists" cared to vote than did the "planners only". Now, out of the architect-planners, more than 40% were in private practice in 1962. However, of 384 architectural firms doing town planning work which had replied to Anthony Goss' questionnaire, for over 50% town planning accounted for 10% or less of their work.[28] It is reasonable to expect that a considerable proportion of double-qualified architect-planners working in these firms did *not* bother to vote.

A low voting turn-out of architect planners could thus be understandable in terms of the *occupational environment* in which they dominated and which, on the whole, might have induced them to regard the question as not quite as important as the establishments of the TPI and RIBA had assumed. Other "specialists" might have been even less

[27]The Town Planning Institute, Current Trends in the Town Planning Institute's Member and Associate Classes, *Journal of the Town Planning Institute*, Vol. 53, June 1967, pp. 245-6.

[28]Goss, *op. cit.*, p. 35.

concerned from the beginning. Their professional associations were less involved in this conflict than the RIBA was, and recruitment from the other parent professions into town planning had dwindled to less than ten per year during the decade preceding the conflict:

Summary of Election to Associate Membership during decades[29]

	1956–66	1946–56	1936–46
Direct entry planners	494	250	34
	39.8%	22.2%	7.6%
Architects	341	512	229
	27.5%	45.4%	51.2%
Engineers	56	162	108
	4.5%	14.3%	24.2%
Surveyors	86	101	38
	6.9%	9.1%	8.45%
Other degrees (geographers, economists, sociologists, etc.)	262	101	38
	22.5%	9.1%	8.45%
Totals	1239	1126	447

The issue of "generalists" versus "specialists" was thus one mainly between the representatives of the RIBA in the TPI and those of its corporate members whom I have described as "planners only". These "planners only", however, had their stronghold in local planning authorities, as the following considerations show:

To start with, it is known from the Goss Report that, in 1962, architect-planners made for only 22% of all local authority appointments held by chartered town planners in Great Britain. The figures for the other two specialist groups are unfortunately not known, but their absolute numbers are much smaller. Allowing even for the possibility of a substantially larger proportion of engineer-planners and surveyor-planners than architect-planners having been in local government service, the proportion of all "specialists" in local government could have been not more than 60% in 1962. Given the low recruitment figures for engineers and surveyors and the high recruitment figures for "planners only" during 1956–66 documented above, this proportion is bound to have declined

[29] Current Trends, *op. cit.*

sharply thereafter, assuming, that is, that architects have continued to stay clear of local authority work. The following is an estimate for 1962 and 1965, based on available evidence about recruitment:

	1962*	in %	Recruitment 1962–65**	1965	in %
Architect-planners	310	22	36	346	19
Engineer-planners) Surveyor-planners)	536	38	39	575	33
Planners only	765	40	90	855	48
Totals	1611	100	165	1776	100

* Figure for architect-planners and total based on Goss; estimate for other "specialists" based on their low total in 1965 (786).

** Assuming that 30% of architects, 60% of "planners only" and virtually *all* the other "specialists" have gone into LAs.

It must be emphasised that the assumption of only 60% of the newly recruited "planners only" going into local planning authorities is very conservative indeed. It is based on the assumption of the distribution of "planners only" between different employment categories being similar to that of *all* planners in 1962. As a matter of fact, most of the other fields were domains more of the architect-planners than anybody else. The figures quoted by Goss[30] are the following:

Employment	Number of planners in 1962	in %	% of Architects in employment category	Architects in %
Local Government	1411	60	22	32
Private practice	483	21	80	41
Central Government	223	9	48	10
New Towns and other public bodies	108	5	72	10
Teaching	77	3	72	5
Other	46	2	61	2
Totals	2348	100	—	100

[30] Goss, *op. cit.*

The proportion of newly recruited "planners only" going into local planning authorities could therefore have been more nearly 80%, which gives a reasonable margin of error and still allows one to infer that, at the time of the decisive vote, at least 50% of all chartered town planners in local government *must have been what has been described as "planners only"*.

Why should these have had grievances against the "specialists", grievances which probably induced them to take a strong attitude on the policies suggested by the Council? It has been suggested that the "revolt" of the "planners only" could be linked to chances of promotion to chief-officer. This motivation is *well-founded in the actual situation*, and it applied to planners in local government more than anybody else. The next table gives the qualifications of "Local Government Officers responsible for Planning in England and Wales" in 1950/1[31] and 1963/4.[32]

Planners only	6	4.2	8	5.5
Specialist planners*	76	53.2	93	64.7
Specialist only (no planning qualification)	61	42.6	43	29.8
Total	143	100	144	100

* Planners with other qualifications.

This shows that — although the proportion of chief officers with planning qualifications increased quite considerably — this increase *benefited almost exclusively the "specialist" planners*, i.e. architect-planners, engineer-planners and surveyor-planners, thus throwing new light on the demands quoted earlier that the double-qualification requirement for chief officer grades should be dropped. This is because the figures clearly suggest a widespread practice on the part of local authorities of reserving such posts for "specialist" planners. The "planners only" in local government must have had the feeling that their way to the top posts was blocked by the "specialists".

[31]P. Collison, Qualifications of Planning Officers, *The Builder*, Vol. 187, September 24, 1954, p. 501.

[32]The Town Planning Institute, *Year Book 1964*, quoted after Stringer, *op. cit.*

Some additional figures allow one to indulge in more speculation. The figures quoted above show that there were only eight "planners only" amongst the ranks of chief planning officers in 1963/4. But the Goss Report quotes the number of 43 for chief officers *and deputies* in local planning authorities for 1962. This means that far more deputy chief planning officers than chief planning officers were "planners only". As K. Deutsch suggests, men who are just below the top (such as colonels) are in unique positions to engineer revolts because they are close enough to the rank-and-file membership to gauge its feeling, and close enough to the top to gain an overview over the total situation.[33] To prove that this has been the case in 1965 would require personal interviews and research efforts beyond the scope of this paper, but the situation was such that some deputies would have had a motivation for organising the resistance of the "planners only". And there was at least some organised effort behind it: there were busloads of rank-and-file members coming to the Extraordinary General Meeting in January 1965, and somebody must have chartered those buses.

It must finally be added that the predominance of the *"specialist" was also reflected in the Institute's membership structure itself.*[34] Thus, the *percentage of members (as against associate members) was twice as high for the "specialists"*:

	Associate members		Members		Members as % of whole group	
Architects	38.5%		34.8%		14.7%	
Engineers	11.7%		23.5%		27.7%	
Surveyors	8.0%		17.5%		29.3%	
"Specialists"		58.2%		75.8%		19.9%
Direct-entry	27.2%		15.5%		9.7%	
Other degrees	14.6%		8.7%		11.4%	
"Planners only"		41.8%		24.2%		9.9%
Total	100%	100%	100%	100%		

---

[33] K. W. Deutsch, *The Nerves of Government – Models of Political Communication and Control*, 2nd ed., New York – London 1966, pp. 155-6.

[34] Current Trends, *op. cit.*

Associate Members and Members not only had differential status within the Institute, there was also a substantial difference in power: the Council consisted mainly of Members and only few Associate Members (together with representatives of other membership classes such as Legal Members, etc.) so that the "specialists" making for 76% of the membership class were bound to dominate the Council of the TPI. The results in terms of a predominance of the "specialists" were striking: At the time of the conflict, *of 39 Council Members* (Members and Associate Members without representation of other classes) *35 were members of other professional institutes and only four "planners only ".*[35]

Thus, although no specific data are available to demonstrate the point itself, all indications are that the rejection of the Resolution of the Council proposing a broadening of the membership of the TPI by including the "contributors" to the planning process was the result of what may be called a "revolt" by the "planners only".

One may add to this that the reality of planning work in many of the local planning authorities — especially the smaller ones — may *actually have resembled the "generalist" concept* of the planner's role. Staffing and resources simply do not allow for teamwork in the same way as operated by consultancies and Development Corporations. Thus, the interpretation that the *majority of local government planning staff voted "generalist" becomes persuasive.*

To summarise:

(a) There was ill-feeling between "specialists" and "planners only" prior to the events of 1964/5.

(b) The ill-feeling was stronger in local government where the "planners only" had their stronghold.

(c) Animosity was linked with the chances of promotion to chief planning officers, a point which could have been of special interest to a number of deputies who were "planners only".

(d) The irritation of "planners only" was augmented by the disproportionate share which the "specialists" held of the membership class and of seats on the Council of the TPI.

It remains to be shown that this revolt was actually the direct result of

[35]The Town Planning Institute, *Year Book 1964—65.* Some of these were *ex-officio* members and not elected.

the implementation of most of the Schuster Committee's proposals. An analysis of the number of members elected per year clearly bears this out. After the Schuster Report was published the "specialists" quickly lost ground whereas "planners only" gained tremendously, as the following table shows: [36]

	1936/45	1946/55	1956/65	1968	1969	1970
"Specialists"	84%	68%	38%	43%	29%	27%
"Planners only"	16%	32%	62%	57%	71%	73%

The effect of the Schuster Report is clearly shown on the following chart: [37]

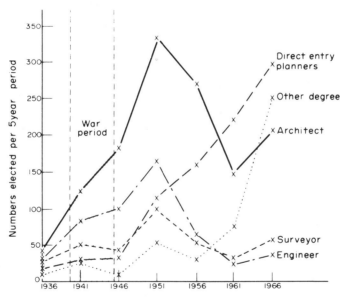

Chart showing changes in rates of election to associate members

[36]Figures for 1936–1965 after Current Trends, *op. cit.*, the figures for 1968, 1969 and 1970 were kindly supplied by Mr. Herd, Education Officer of the Royal Town Planning Institute.

[37]Current Trends, *op. cit.*

Between 1956 and 1961 the "direct entry" planners surpassed architects, and in 1961/6 architects only ranked third after "direct entry" and "other degrees". In the case of architects this is not even due to a significant loss in actual numbers of entrants but rather to the very conspicuous increase of "planners only", especially in the "other degrees" category, i.e. graduates who have qualified via Graduate Courses in Town Planning. Their number started climbing with the exemption of geographers and economists from the Intermediate Examination, i.e. after 1953. Recent figures suggest that the increase of "other degrees" amongst the "planners only" is due to a tremendous influx of graduates in *geography* in particular into postgraduate courses granting full exemption from the TPI's Final Examination: in 1969, geographers formed the largest single source of recruitment; in 1970 they were only marginally out-numbered by "direct entry planners".[38]

This has been the history of the "specialist" vs. "generalist" conflict. After the resolution early in 1965 a new Council was elected which subsequently adopted a "generalist" line. What should be evident by now is that this was not primarily a conflict over alternative interpretations of the planner's professional role, and desirable qualifications for it, but rather over *professional interests*. This applies, obviously, to both sides: The "generalist" as much as the "specialist" line both reflect hard facts of life such as promotion chances, access to power, demarcation disputes inside local authorities etc., and are to this extent *ideological*.

[38]From information supplied by Mr. Herd.

British Planning Education: The Changing Scene

This essay is concerned with changes in British planning education occurring between the mid-sixties and the mid-seventies, a period during which town planning established its professional identity only to be faced with confusing and threatening changes in its context. This challenge, and the responses to it, reverberated throughout the planning schools during the more than five years that I was at the Oxford Polytechnic.

Before describing these developments, there are a few concepts which might confuse the non-British reader as they confused me when I first came to Britain. The most important one for understanding British planning education is that of a *profession*. The development of the professions in Britain has been the object of a thorough study by Millerson (1964). Briefly, with virtually no state-regulation of their activities in 19th century Britain, practitioners of certain high-level skills felt the urgent need to protect their reputation, and ultimately their interests, against the impression created by malpractices. They formed what Millerson aptly described as qualifying associations. Members of these were supposed to have attained a certain level of qualification, adhere to a code of conduct and to a scale of professional fees.

Insistence on a certain level of professional competence soon led to *entrance examinations*. It is important to realise that these were initially a purely professional affair and did not form part of any educational system. This is underlined by the fact that they are often termed *external* examinations. Still nowadays, it is possible for anybody with certain minimum educational attainments to take such external examinations and to join many of the professions. Membership of a profession is, firstly, almost a pre-requisite of practising it and, secondly, puts the person concerned, for most intents and purposes, on *a par* with a university graduate.

A factor which contributed to nineteenth-century professions concentrating on the qualifications of their members is that, unlike on the

Continent with its many polytechnic schools, British higher education had originally neglected technical education. When the education sector began to develop an interest, the professions were the well-established authorities for granting professional qualifications in this field. However, the smaller professions in particular found it very difficult indeed to provide the necessary facilities for obtaining them, and a form of cooperation between the professions and the higher education sector emerged which is absent on the Continent: the so-called *recognised schools* system. What it means is that the graduates from certain specified courses offered at institutions of higher education are exempted from all, or parts of, the external examinations of most of the professions. It is obvious that this gives the professions control over course development so that, whenever planning educators used to meet during my time in Britain, the Royal Town Planning Institute was present in their discussions as the, largely unseen, villain of the piece against whose apparently absurd policies they objected.

Next to explaining some features of professions and professionalism, one must deal with higher education itself. Here, the key-point is that not every British degree, and consequently not every course, offers a professional qualification. As against continental higher education, where the idea is clearly that of every graduate being able to enter into practice of some kind more or less straight after graduation, the idea of a British undergraduate degree based on the model of "Oxbridge" (Oxford–Cambridge, the two oldest English universities) is more that of "educating the gentleman" who could subsequently "learn on the job", if need should be. Consequently, courses for British *undergraduate* degrees are much shorter than continental university courses — usually three years. They are augmented by a whole array of *postgraduate* courses providing further qualifications. Sometimes, such courses are termed *graduate* (as against postgraduate), when they introduce holders of undergraduate degrees to a new area of concern instead of building on their previous degree. Finally, there are certain exceptions to the rule of three-year undergraduate courses. Courses which attempt to combine the liberal education rationale of the three-year course with the aim of providing a professional qualification last longer. Architecture and town planning provide examples of these.

The situation is complicated still further by the fact that British higher education has two sectors, *polytechnics* and *universities*, with the first generally aspiring to the status of the second. In this, they are encouraged by successive governments hoping to reduce the costs of higher education overall by providing more "education on the cheap" in the generally, in terms of finance and facilities, more impoverished polytechnics. Oxford Polytechnic is one of them. During the period covered by this paper, it succeeded in attaining a reasonable degree of parity with universities, signified by the fact that it now awards academic degrees. At the same time, its planning qualifications (formerly diplomas, now degrees) exempt their holders from the Royal Town Planning Institute's external examination.

With these explanations it is hoped that the following account will be easier for a non-British reader to understand. This is because the (now Royal) Town Planning Institute as one of a whole array of professional organisations behaved in exactly the way described above. Education in town planning had been one of its prime concerns since its foundation in 1914. Like others, it had devised a system of external examinations in 1916 and operated it since 1920. This, and the granting of exemptions from its Final Examination to graduates of recognised schools, were and still are the vehicles of its educational policy. In its early days only members of one of the "parent professions", architecture, engineering and surveying, were eligible to take the Institute's Final Examination. It consisted of three papers on matters of planning *per se* (including a sketch plan and report), and three on the relations of town planning with the parent professions and with law. The parent professions extended their influence even further through the formation of the Joint Examination Board in 1931. However, at the same time an Intermediate Examination was introduced enabling entrants for the first time to become professionally qualified in planning only. A qualification in one of the parent professions became tantamount to exemption from the Institute's Intermediate Examination.

The importance of creating an Intermediate Examination was only to emerge after World War II. In 1951 the Schuster Committee (HMSO, 1950) recommended that town planning, being a matter not merely of physical design but of social and economic policy, should be open to all graduates. The Town Planning Institute responded cautiously by exempting economists and geographers from its Intermediate Examination in 1953. In 1963, the privilege was extended to sociologists. The main effect was to open the doors for a great influx of geographers into planning.*

It was partly the desire to redress the balance amongst newly qualified planners between geographers and the parent professions which motivated the Council of the Town Planning Institute (almost completely dominated by the parent professions) to create a "Special Committee on Membership and Recruitment" in the early sixties. The latter proposed a scheme for the Final Examination which was to give all candidates an understanding of the basic principles and practice of planning and, besides, to allow them to take an advanced test in their specialism. In effect it suggested to make entry into town planning easier for members of the parent professions. This position was subsequently termed "specialist" (Faludi, 1972) to distinguish it from the "generalist" view of planning as a profession in its own right.

In terms of the recognised schools policy, the implications of this move were never considered properly. There existed two types of courses: firstly, such accepting entrants qualified in one of the parent professions and, since 1953, also graduates in many other disciplines and, secondly, courses on undergraduate level. Probably, the implications of the "specialists" carrying the day in 1965 would have been for undergraduate courses to develop only slowly, and for the others to diversify greatly with individual courses catering for entrants from specific professions, this possibly in close association with their own prestigious schools.

However, the opposing "generalists" rather than the "specialists" prevailed and rejected the attempt to lower the threshold for entry by members of the parent professions rescinding even such privileges as architects, engineers and surveyors, and incidentally also geographers, had enjoyed up until then. A new Education Committee proposed a "Revised Scheme for the Final Examination" (The Town Planning Institute, 1967) complementing the profession's newly formed view of physical planning as a distinct area of professional concern rather than as an area of further specialisation for members of the parent professions. In terms of the recognised schools policy, the Town Planning Institute came to favour undergraduate courses, though not to the exclusion of what were now to

*Subsequently, these were to side with the "direct entry" planners to argue the generalist case. See the previous essay.

be termed graduate courses.* This was because, in the words of the then Chairman of the Education Committee, the "... test of the planning profession's claim to a distinct field of activity is the practicability of framing an undergraduate educational programme" (Kantorowich, 1967). This view, together with an estimated shortage of qualified town planners running into several thousands which the Town Planning Institute had envisaged for some time (The Town Planning Institute, 1964) and which it emphasised in its evidence to the Committee on the Staffing of Local Government (HMSO, 1967b), led it to pursue its policy of expanding undergraduate planning education. The Institute made representations to the Ministry for Housing and Local Government and the Ministry of Education to increase the number of courses during the next quinquennium then under consideration by the University Grants Committee. These were successful, and university courses in planning expanded. In addition, undergraduate courses were also established in the growing number of polytechnics, initially as diploma courses, but increasingly leading to degrees awarded under the auspices of the Council of National Academic Awards. For all these courses now numbering well over a dozen (as well as for graduate courses, both full-time and part-time) the new Final Examination syllabus acted as a yardstick. Although intended as a minimum standard, its extensive coverage and its rigorous application in granting recognition, in particular to the newly emerging courses, tended to exert pressure towards uniformity of planning education which planning educators and close observers have complained about ever since (e.g. Cockburn, 1970c; Progress in Planning, 1973).

The new Final Examination syllabus of the Royal Town Planning Institute was prepared in outline by the Education Committee in 1965/7, accepted in this form by the Council in May 1967, worked out in detail in 1967/9, published in April 1969 (The Town Planning Institute, 1969) and brought into operation in 1970.

The generalist concept underlying this syllabus was particularly relevant to the context of traditional British local government with relatively rigid boundaries between departments. In this environment town planning was a newcomer. Many authorities did not even have a separate department of

---

*To distinguish them from, in terms of planning, truly postgraduate courses for qualified planners.

planning but joint ones for architecture and planning, engineering and planning, etc. Having been the target of, as the majority of town planners saw it, a take-over bid from architects as the most powerful of the professions operating in their vicinity and wanting to make access to a town planning qualification easier for architects, planners reacted by emphasising their distinctiveness. What they intended was to convince themselves and others that physical planning above the scale of individual buildings involved a separate skill, one which justified separate departments of planning, separate career structures, including chief planning officer posts, for which candidates needed no other qualification than one in town planning; and a separate educational system. This is what the "generalist" concept seemed to justify, hence its adoption. Nobody seemed to mind that, rather than being generalist, the concept simply meant a bid for recognition of physical planning as a new specialism.

The origin of the "generalist" concept in a territorial dispute within local government is well illustrated by a diagram on the "role of contributors" in an article by one of its most articulate proponents (Kantorowich, 1967). It shows " the planning process" taking place in the "planner's office". My purpose will now be to show that the context of town planning is changing to the extent of considerably modifying the meaning of that phrase "the planner's office". To take account of these changes, the planning profession has meanwhile reopened the debate on the role of the planner.

The stages by which changes have occurred are marked by a series of official reports starting from the Maud and Mallaby Report (HMSO 1967a,b) on the management and staffing of local government. These were significant not so much for the quality of their argument (Stanyer, 1970) but for the official blessing which they gave to a great deal of experimentation in local government. Since their publication, local government has been on the move.

Just one year later the secretary of the Association of Municipal Corporations reported on massive changes taking place (Swaffield, 1968). They concerned the introduction of new management procedures and other devices for streamlining policy making and administration. The general intention was to make local government internally more coherent than hitherto. This was enforced by the Seebohm Report (HMSO, 1968b) on the social services published the same year.

For the following years, public attention focused more on the spectacular reform of the powers and boundaries of local government than on its internal make-up. However, the Maud Commission's report on local government reform (HMSO, 1969) still incorporated basic tenets of the previous ones. At the same time, reorganisation continued in various authorities with the report on Liverpool Corporation by a firm of international management consultants and the re-structuring of Coventry's administration providing two conspicuous examples. Also, academic institutions took a specific interest in local government reform, with the Institute for Local Government Studies at the University of Birmingham taking a lead.

The next official report in this series *Transport Planning – The Men For The Job* (HMSO, 1970) spelt it out to town planners that the days of separate departments might soon be over. It insisted that, in future, there should be large departments of land use and transport rather like the social services departments to be introduced in the wake of the Seebohm Report in 1971. The link with transport is indeed the most plausible one that needs to be forged by physical planners and one which has been accepted as Town Planning Institute policy since.

The next official report on internal reorganisation, the Bains Report (HMSO, 1972), as well as various publications coming out of the Institute for Local Government Studies (for instance: Stewart, 1971; Eddison, 1973) with its courses for middle and top-level administrators which by now many of those concerned with local government reorganisation must have attended, show the trend remaining the same as indicated; local government is different in several important ways rendering the generalist concept obsolete. Planning will cease to be the concern of individual departments with their profusion of unco-ordinated planning which has prompted Stewart (1969a) to complain about too much rather than too little planning in local government; it will attend to the linkages between the areas of concern of existing departments; it will differentiate between a more general and more operational level. The greatest challenges in planning will therefore arise outside that type of local government which planners aspired to set up for themselves in the middle-sixties and for which the generalist concept was tailor-made. Certainly, for all that one knows about procedures in the emergent form of local government it seems that there will be new forms of planning going beyond town and country planning. Rather than giving any profession, discipline, or department a *prima facie* responsibility for planning in each single area, there will be co-operative styles of work, the binding element between departments (if indeed there are departments) being common planning procedures.

For town planners to be successful in this broader form of planning, they will have to go back on the very concept which has given them such a tremendous impetus for securing their positions in local government and for expanding the numerical strength of their profession. This process, which is well under way, is the development to which I now turn.

This development began at the end of the last decade when Eddison (1968) and Stewart (1969a,b) first gave their interpretations of the 1968 Town and Country Planning Act against changing views of local government and Amos (1969) spoke about the general planning function. This was followed by the Centre for Environmental Studies taking an interest in planning education which had always been closely related to the issues of membership policy and the role of the planner. It published three studies (Cockburn, 1970a,b) and assembled a working party on objectives for planning education which published its report only recently (Progress in Planning, 1973). The chairman of the working party was Amos, then Senior Vice President of the Town Planning Institute and lined up for President in 1971/2.

The orientation of this working party, as well as that of the previous Centre for Environmental Studies publications, was toward the broader concept of planning deploring the relatively heavy investment in town planning education at the expense of planning in other fields. It was this question of the relationship between town planning and emergent forms of planning which must have prompted the Town Planning Institute in 1970 to publish a discussion note on *The Changing Shape of the Planning Process*. It argued the case for the planning profession getting involved in the new, broader form of planning (The Town Planning Institute, 1970). This was followed by a conference sponsored by the Membership Committee of the Town Planning Institute where Amos put the case for widening the membership and permitting a greater degree of specialisation in planning education (The Town Planning Institute, 1971). In his Presidential Address (Amos, 1971) the same year he stated that ". . . the Institute's current posture concentrates attention upon the application of the planning process to physical planning at various scales, to the exclusion of direct applications of the process to social and economic phenomena and to the neglect of management planning of coincident physical, social and economic factors". During his presidency, the Royal Town Planning Institute then published a much more extensive Discussion Paper on *Town Planners and their Future* (The Royal Town Planning Institute, 1971). It set out five "alternative futures" (two with two variants each) for the Institute, its membership and educational policy, this against the background of a set of assumptions about changes in local government similar to those outlined earlier in this chapter. The stillborn "Learned Society" alternative apart, these form a continuum from the most inclusive "Institute of Planning" to retaining the Institute in its existing shape. All options, except for the last, had a ring of the rejected "specialist" position of the early sixties about them in so far as they emphasised diversity over unity in the profession. The difference was that the identity of town planning as a profession was not threatened from any one source. Rather, some more diffuse developments had changed the entire planning scene making diversification more pallatable.

The membership opted for a variant of the most obvious alternative termed "Institute for Environmental Planning 2". It thus responded to pressures for change, but only cautiously, staying well clear of the more adventurous schemes embracing other than physical forms of planning. As regards the broader form of planning (variously termed the "organisation planning field" or "corporate management" in the Discussion Paper) the position of the Institute sketched in that document was not unlike that of its own parent professions before it itself had come of age: it proposed to join other professional societies to "further knowledge and advance training" in it.

For planning education the line suggested is however clearly more sensible than hitherto. Rather than exercising rigid control over virtually the whole of the curriculum, the Institute will now only concern itself with core studies lasting for two years out of the four to five years of higher education which a qualified planner must have. For the rest, there is "freedom for innovation", as the document puts it, indicating at the same time that these years could be taken up by "scale" studies (regional, local, etc.) or by "subject" studies (transport, economics, design, etc.).

The underlying logic is that of the "generalist-with-a-specialism" which

Perloff (1957) developed in his classic on *Education for Planning*. However, this is applied to "environmental planning" only. We are told that all town planners should have ". . . a common core of professional expertise underlying one of a series of specialisations". The core, it is said, would consist of: "(a) planning methodology, (b) knowledge and understanding of the physical environment within which planning takes place, and (c) knowledge and understanding of the relevant administrative context and organisation". Beyond this, educational institutions would be encouraged to "develop reputations for particular aspects", i.e. either subject areas or planning scales as mentioned above. This is on the assumption that "practical realities mean that not all planners will be able to do every job in planning".

Currently, the Institute continues along these lines. Yet another Discussion Paper (The Royal Town Planning Institute, 1973) proposed a "modular" approach to planning courses combining "foundation" and "applied" courses. As regards the more general form of planning it emphasises the value of "post-qualification" courses. This has become official policy since (The Royal Town Planning Institute, 1974).

Now, one may criticise this scheme, as I have done implicitly in the penultimate essay in this volume, for not taking the "generalist-with-a-specialism" logic far enough by altogether omitting the part of the core course relating to the physical environment and bringing forward the wider aspects of planning to be taught in subsequent post-qualification courses. However, politics, including professional politics, is the art of the possible. The compromise between the aspirations of the high fliers of the profession and the need for relative security on part of its rank and file which this package represents is all that one could get, at this stage anyway. It signals the abandonment of one of the pretences of the old generalist concept – that every planner should be capable of covering the total field of physical planning. It also takes cognisance of the wider form of planning developing in local government without attempting to embrace it. In particular, it opens the doors for experimentation and variety in British planning education. More precisely, it legitimises the variety which already exists under the blanket cover of recognition by the Institute.

References

AMOS, F. J. C. (1971) The development of the planning process, *Journal of the Royal Town Planning Institute*, Vol. 57, pp. 304-8.

COCKBURN, C. (1970a) Facts about planning courses, *Information Papers*, No. 14, Centre for Environmental Studies, London.

COCKBURN, C. (1970b) The provision of planning education, *Information Papers*, No. 15, Centre for Environmental Studies, London.

COCKBURN, C. (1970c) Opinion and planning education, *Information Papers*, No. 21, Centre for Environmental Studies, London.

EDDISON, T. (1968) The wider role of the development plan, *Journal of the Town Planning Institute*, Vol. 54, pp. 465-67.

EDDISON, T. (1973) *Local Government: Management and Corporate Planning*, Leonard Hill, Aylesbury, Bucks.

FALUDI, A. (1972) The "specialist" versus "generalist" conflict, *Oxford Working Papers in Planning Education and Research*, No. 12, Oxford Polytechnic, Oxford. (For an excerpt see the second essay in this volume.)

HMSO (1950) *Qualification of Planners* (Schuster Report) London.

HMSO (1967a) *Management of Local Government* (Maud Committee) London.

HMSO (1967b) *Staffing of Local Government* (Mallaby Committee) London.

HMSO (1968b) *Report of the Committee on Local Authority and Allied Personal Social Services* (Seebohm Committee) London.

HMSO (1969) *Report of the Royal Commission of Local Government in England* (Maud Commission) London.

HMSO (1970) *Transport Planning: The Men For The Job: A Report to the Minister of Transport by Lady Sharp*, London.

HMSO (1972) *The New Local Authorities: Management and Structure* (Bains Committee) London.

KANTOROWICH, R. H. (1967) Education for planning, *Journal of the Town Planning Institute*, Vol. 53, pp. 175-184.

MILLERSON, G. (1964) *The Qualifying Associations*, Routledge & Kegan Paul, London.

PERLOFF, H. S. (1957) *Education for Planning – City, State and Regional*, Johns Hopkins, Baltimore.

PROGRESS IN PLANNING (1973) *Education for Planning*, Report of a Working Group at the Centre for Environmental Studies, Vol. 1, Pergamon, Oxford, pp. 1-108.

STEWART, J. D. (1969a) The administrative structure of planning: 1, *Journal of the Town Planning Institute*, Vol. 55, pp. 288-90.

STEWART, J. D. (1969b) The case for local authority policy planning, *Town and Country Planning Summer School Nottingham*, 1969 (Conference Proceedings) The Town Planning Institute, London.

STEWART, J. D. (1971) *Management in Local Government: A Viewpoint*, Charles Knight, London.

SWAFFIELD, J. C. (1968) Local government changing, *New Society*, 19 September, p. 407.

THE ROYAL TOWN PLANNING INSTITUTE (1973) *Town Planners and their Future – Implications of Changes in Education and Membership Policy: A Further Discussion Paper*, London.

THE ROYAL TOWN PLANNING INSTITUTE (1974) Education Policy: guidelines for Planning Schools, *The Planner*, Vol. 60, pp. 802-8.

THE TOWN PLANNING INSTITUTE (1964) *Membership Policy: A Memorandum by the Council to all Corporate Members*, London.

THE TOWN PLANNING INSTITUTE (1967) Revised scheme for the final examination, *Progress Report on Membership Policy*, London.

THE TOWN PLANNING INSTITUTE (1969) *Examinations Handbook*, London.

THE TOWN PLANNING INSTITUTE (1970) *The Changing Shape of the Planning Process – A TPI Discussion Note*, London.

THE TOWN PLANNING INSTITUTE (1971) *One Day Membership Policy Conference*, University of Manchester, 24 February

Part II

From the Work-bench of Planning Education

Planning theory relates directly to problems experienced in planning practice, especially those arising during any attempt to make and take decisions rationally. Since it is in project work that planning education comes closest to elucidating these problems, the teaching of planning theory must relate to it. The planning theorist on a planning course cannot afford to stay aloof from its, albeit simulated, practice element. On the contrary, he must work on this "coal-face" of planning education. (He must also concern himself with matters of curriculum development and course planning, and with the general problems arising out of the felt need on planning courses to integrate disciplines around the core-ideas of planning, matters which will concern us in Part III of this volume.)

The two essays in Part II represent examples of various reports which I wrote from the work-bench of planning education. The first one (on which, incidentally, Chapter 14 of my previous work on *Planning Theory* is based) is more programmatic in setting out the principles of project work as I see them. They have developed with little fundamental change since. Thus, projects designed by the Planning Theory Group at Delft University of Technology still show features of the "Witney project" on which this paper was based.* The central point of project work, as far as planning theory is concerned, is that of arriving at an operational definition of the planning process in its political context and in the face of complexity and uncertainty. The educational vehicle by which to achieve this is a combination of advance theoretical discussion, the attempt to engage in an exercise in rational planning in an, albeit simulated, context which reflects the diversity of the planner's clientele, and a period of structured reflection at the end of the project. "Mini-projects" introduced

*For an English version of our project brief see the appendix in G. Crispin (1975).

before the initial "thinking" phase so as to provide a basis for discussing the operational problems of planning, and a manual on how to approach planning problems (Planning Theory Group, 1975) setting out the basic principles and criticisms of rational planning with exercises and readings based on Friend and Jessop, Simon, Etzioni, Altshuler, Chadwick and Popper as a guide for the two theoretical phases of projects are but further extensions of these principles.

The second essay in Part II represents a different kind of message from the work-bench of planning education. It should give evidence of the capacity of project work to become a laboratory in which to try out some modestly innovatory ideas, such as that of structuring the action space of a decision-taker into concentric zones of feasibility and of limiting the initial search for the preferred alternative to the zone of highest feasibility. As the paper explains, this represents a response to the, theoretically as well as practically speaking, perennial problem of planning: information overload.

At the same time, this paper is representative of the challenges and responses which occur in education. Having worked with morphological analysis previously (amongst others in the project on which the first paper was based), and having introduced Analysis of Interconnected Decision Areas as a superior approach in the project under consideration, it became necessary to link the two together by describing them in a generalised language which, furthermore, complemented the theoretical directions I had set out in published works. The attempt made in "*Action space analysis*" also indicates a direction in which I hope to move in the future, that of relating the strategic choice approach (of which AIDA is a central technique) more closely to the theory of rational planning.

The student report in the appendix to the second essay represents an example of the high standard which is often attained under the hot-house conditions of project work. It is included partly in recognition of the contribution which this and other student groups have made to the development of my thinking.

References

CRISPIN, G. (1975) Project work in education for urban and regional planning, *Working Papers in Planning Theory and Education*, nr. 4, Vereniging voor Studie- en Studentenbelangen te Delft.

PLANNING THEORY GROUP (1975) *De Aanpak van Projekten*, mimeo, Delft University of Technology.

Teaching the Planning Process *

Educational planning projects are beset by one problem: lack of feedback resulting from the absence of a real-life community reacting through its many-faceted agencies to the challenges of a planning proposal. This makes it difficult to give students a realistic experience of the planning process.

Various attempts have been made to overcome this problem. In traditional planning projects, students are following fairly specific planning briefs and, at the end of the day, they are judged by their tutors and/or outside experts on how closely their attempt resembles a piece of professional work, with the real world context being provided, for better or for worse, by the accumulated experience of their judges. In "live projects", students descend on a community for a limited period of time, engaging it in a mock-planning exercise, thus giving, possibly, a sense of realism. In games, participants interact with a highly abstract model of the environment, receiving instant feedback as to the effects of their decisions and thus experiencing planning as a process.

The project on which I am reporting is in some way a mixture between the traditional approach and a game. It has attempted to combine the close resemblance to a well-defined piece of professional work[1] with the facility of feedback offered by simulation. Only, instead of building a model of the environment we have built a fairly abstract model of the "socio-political process", and let it interact with our planning proposals.

An Approach to Project Work

With this combination, I have tried to give students a sense of the way in which experts operate in a political environment. Beyond this, I

*My thanks are to my colleagues amongst staff and students of the Department of Town Planning, Oxford Polytechnic, who have helped me in making the experiences reported in this paper. The diagrams have been drawn by Robert Baker.

generally try to observe a number of points in project work: first, I hold that structuring one's approach to problem-solving often requires a greater amount of creative thinking than the *minutiae* of operating techniques. It is therefore important that projects should largely be self-guided, despite the conflicts which this may generate, and on which I have reported elsewhere.[2] The form which self-guidance takes is that of a steering group with rotating membership. They write briefs for individual groups during each phase, they coordinate and they turn the wheels of the sometimes quite complex administrative machinery servicing a project.

Secondly, I take the view that assessment of projects is best related to the objectives set for each group and that staff and students should be involved in this process of "management by objectives" collectively, although again this is not without problems.[3]

Lastly, in a project of any degree of complexity, time must be set aside for thinking, so as to increase its effectiveness as an educational process. The initial phase is therefore devoted mainly to grappling with general problems of the planning process, of planning methodology, and the more philosophical questions underlying it. By the same token, the last phase is, as a matter of course, devoted to "reflection", that is, to summarising what has been learned, criticising one's achievements, and to suggesting improvements.

In dealing with the planning process during project work, I am finally concerned with neither facts nor techniques, except in so far as they are necessary for demonstrating what is essential about planning. As regards facts, I am quite content to accept unreliable information. As regards techniques, the simplest ones should do. Techniques become obsolete almost as rapidly as one acquires them. It is the analysis of techniques and their use which is far more important than the accumulation of a great fund of experience in operating them.

Concepts of the Planning Process (Fig. 1)

There are three points to be made about concepts of the planning process which we developed during the initial "thinking" phase. One is that it is an intentionally rational procedure of problem-solving, and that it must therefore, by and large, generate and evaluate alternative plans.

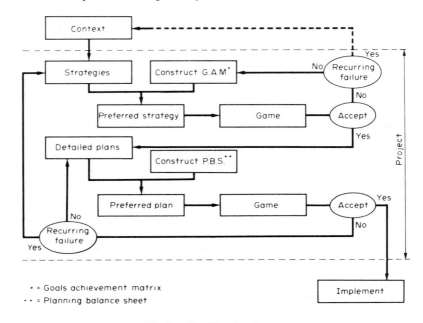

Fig. 1   The Planning Process.

Secondly, we came to think of planning as an iterative process — planners and a community agreeing on a preferred course of action over a set of plans. Here, we tried to avoid mechanistic ideas on goal-setting, that is, that goals are set by the socio-political process and then translated into action programmes by planners. We rather stipulated: (a) that the type of problem to which a Town Map addressed itself was circumscribed by statutory powers reflecting goals of a general kind, that is, that physical development should be controlled; (b) that some of the substantive ends of our plan[4] had been set on a county-wide level — and quite rightly so; and (c) that, as for the goals that were to be set within that context, these would be defined by the planners and the socio-political process in close collaboration. It is simply that goals are influenced as much by what is possible as by what is desirable. Technical considerations made by planners, and political considerations made by the elected representative, or the spokesman of a pressure group, should rub off on each other during the planning process.

Finally, we were concerned about how to achieve rationality in spite of the limitations of human problem-solving capacity. Our approach corresponded closely to Etzioni's ideas on "mixed scanning"[5]: we differentiated between a "strategic" and a "detailed" level of problem-solving. Similar to the idea of structure and local plans, this allowed us to concentrate on broad policies first, and to focus on specific problems afterwards leaving ourselves the option of returning to the strategic level as and when required.

The Generation of Alternative Strategies (Figs. 2a to 2d)

Every problem but the most insignificant can be differentiated into a strategic and detailed level with some advantage. There is a very large number of alternatives, even in simple situations. Only by cutting out every possible detail may one be able to define a relatively small number

Fig. 2a, b, c   Housing Parameter – Parametric States

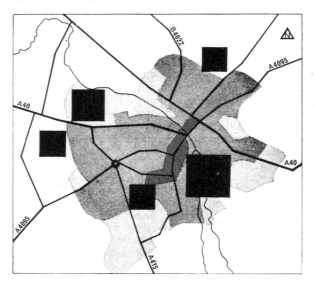

Fig. 2b

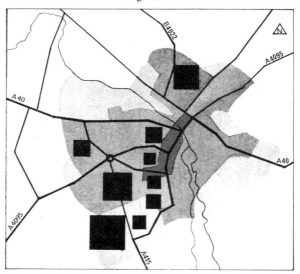

Fig. 2c

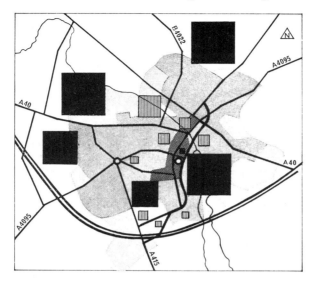

Fig. 2d   The preferred strategy

of conceivable strategies each of which can potentially be developed into a number of more detailed plans.

Beyond this, we had to choose a method by which to generate all conceivable strategies. We opted for "morphological analysis", a method starting from the identification of the "parameters" of any solution, then to proceed by enumerating "parametric states" which these could take, finally to arrive at all conceivable strategies through combination.[6] Out of these, all those are excluded which are incompatible, where the state of one parameter conflicts with that of another.[7]

At the outset, there was obviously uncertainty as to what constituted a strategic parameter. We had to ask ourselves, in each case, whether something would fundamentally affect the final plan or not. The answer might be a straightforward one, or it might emerge only later. In our case it transpired, after some consideration that the employment generated would be relatively insignificant, and that the required acreage could be found, no matter what combination of other parametric states we adopted, so we struck employment from our list of strategic parameters.

In the end we were left with a set of alternative transport patterns, with policies for distributing additional housing in and around the town, and a set of alternatives for shopping. These combined into eighty viable strategies which we put forward for evaluation.

Evaluation of Strategies (Fig. 3)

These strategies indicated very general patterns. Evaluation had to be on a level which was equally general. We chose the simplest form of Morris Hill's "goals of achievement matrix".[8] This assumes: (a) that a plan serves a multitude of goals; (b) that these goals are held by a number of interest groups, and (c) that the incidences of goal achievement as related to those interest groups carry differential weights.

In this simple version, technical evaluation is limited to determining whether a strategy promotes or impedes progress towards a goal or whether that goal remains unaffected. A value of +1, 0, or −1 is inserted into the matrix and this value multiplied with the weight allocated to that particular incidence of goal achievement. The results are then aggregated, giving one overall score for the plan as a whole. Practically speaking this means multiplying two matrices, one representing an assumption concerning the importance attached to certain goals by certain interest groups, their political strength, and any normative assumption concerning the distribution of political influence which one cares to make; the other representing the way in which any particular plan is thought to affect all the goals held by various interest groups forming a community. As one proceeds with evaluating, both assumptions may be improved by varying weights, refining scales of measurement or restructuring matrices depending on incoming information during the testing phase.

Of course, there are the usual problems of aggregating the achievements of goals like amenity and accessibility and economic viability as held by preservationists, car-owners and industrialists respectively. But they all, in order to achieve their goals, trade in one currency which is political influence in a wide sense.[9] All choices concerning a plan are in one sense political choices, for all of them influence is expended, in all cases alternative ways of spending that influence can *not* be taken.

But even so, is it possible to express political influence in numerical

Interest groups	1. Preservation of existing character of town centre	2. Preservation of proximity of countryside	3. Delineation of traffic free areas	4. Elimination of unnecessary traffic from town	5. Provision for industrial expansion	6. Ease of access to new and existing industrial areas	7. Priority of employment interests of residents over newcomers	8. Additional parking spaces for shopping (central area)	9. Avoid development on present open space	10. No severance of residential areas from their services	11. No encroachment on to farmland	12. No industrial estates adjacent to any residential area	13. Upgrading of roads between areas of work, residential, shopping	14. No large new shopping schemes	15. New shopping to be adjacent to present shopping	
Preservationists	−/5	+/2	+/2	+/3												/2
Industrialists					0/4	+/3										/3
Trade Union council							−/9									−/9
Consumers association			+/4					+/4								/8
Sports clubs and associations									0/8							/
Tenants association	0/2		+/2			+/5		+/2								/5
Witney home owners										−/3		−/6				−/9
Witney farmers											−/7					−/7
Witney landowners											−/5	+/3				/2
Witney UDC	0/2			+/2									0/1			/2
Motorists			+/3	+/1				+/2					+/3			/9
Chamber of trade	+/2							+/1						+/3	+/1	/7
																9

Fig. 3 Goals Achievement Matrix

terms? It depends, I think, on the way numbers are used. We tried to look upon our matrices merely as a convenient shorthand for expressing an assumption concerning the intensity with which various interest groups held their goals, and their ability to get them implemented. But clearly, this assumption had to meet the test of leading to a plan which was acceptable to the socio-political process. This is where the iterative process of planners and community agreeing on a plan started.

The "Socio-political" Game

In the absence of a community to talk to we simulated one. The idea was to devise some way by which somebody would talk back to us as regards the manner in which our plan would affect various interest groups. For this we devised a "game" consisting of round after round of voting by representatives of the thirteen "interest groups" which we had identified.[10] Voting was punctuated by clarification of issues by "professional planners", by bargaining sessions and announcement of "scandals" by the local press.

The underlying assumption was that the planning department, on the basis of its appreciation of a situation, including the political context, had come up with a plan which was in effect the strategy having scored highest during the evaluation stage. It had then analysed the plan into contentious issues and put them, together with tentative suggestions as to alternative ways of solving these issues, to the socio-political process to decide. The "game" was simply a way of generating the reaction of this socio-political process within a matter of one morning.

The exercise was effective in promoting skills of communication to a highly critical and sometimes unruly audience of colleagues lacking respect for professional judgement.

There were also remarkable insights into the nature of the socio-political process to be gained even from such a limited exercise. Skilful bargaining, ruthless cheating and filibuster tactics were used. We finally learned to appreciate the importance of agendas when the lunch-hour drew closer!

As it happened the plan withstood all the attacks, thanks mainly to the cunning political manoeuvres of the group representing the county council which we had included as one "interest group", although we had given it the highest number of votes. Had the plan been rejected, we would have gone back to amend our assumptions concerning the distribution of political influence, repeated the evaluation procedure, and presented the socio-political process with another alternative which, so the assumption was, would have suited its set of preferences better than the previous one. After some time, the "best" alternative, best that is in relationship to a particular political constellation, out of the finite number of available strategies, would be found.[11]

Generating Detailed Plans

To generate detailed plans on the basis of our preferred strategy, instead of producing all conceivable solutions, we simply formed four "consultancy groups". This departure was made not for reasons purely of convenience but in order to establish one basic point about "mixed scanning": Once the fundamental strategy has been determined, this framework may be filled in in a less onerous way, that is, by incremental or "bit" decisions.[12]

Evaluation of the four alternatives was then performed using a variation of the planning balance sheet, resulting in their overall ranking. Again, the highest-scoring plan was broken down into contentious issues, alternative solutions to those were outlined, and the whole package submitted to the scrutiny of the socio-political game.[13]

Review of Project

As indicated above, we did review the project, and from this review a thorough report resulted.[14] In what follows I am giving my personal assessment.

We faced a lot of problems during this project, both conceptual and otherwise. There are unresolved issues. Should, after all, goal-setting not come before the other phases of the planning process? Was political influence really a currency which one could express, if only tentatively, in numerical form? Also, as it stands, the project has paid little attention to implementation, although I think it has potential in that respect. One could simulate the socio-political process after a lapse of time, including the direct effect which the plan has on interest groups, with some gaining and some losing in political influence as a result of parts of the plan being implemented.

On the whole, I think it was a rewarding experience for most of us. By balancing our desire to be rational against the limitations of our problem-solving capacity, we did arrive at an operational definition of the rational planning process. We became aware also of the fact that planning techniques are more useful when they provide a structured way of thinking and learning about problems, not only by planners, but also by others participating in the planning process.[15] Lastly, we spent a great deal of time arguing how to approach problems, and comparatively little effort on the search for detailed facts which, after all, were completely ephemeral to the *educational* experience of solving a planning problem!

Notes and References

(1) The project was based on the "Town Map, First Review" for Witney, published by Oxfordshire County Council in May 1968. The target-figure for its development has been set at 20,000 by 1981, as against 10,300 in 1967.

(2) See "Planning projects – Aims and methods", *Forma*, Spring 1971, pp. 7-13.

(3) See my paper on "The assessment of student performance" given at the Planning Teachers Conference at Birmingham in January 1971; see also: "Collective assessment in project work", Oxford Working Papers in Planning Education and Research, No. 2, Oxford 1970.

(4) These were the doubling of population and the building of a bypass. One could compare (a) and (b) with the constraints in a linear programme.

(5) A. Etzioni, "The active society", New York-London 1968.

(6) David Bayliss, "Recent trends in forecasting", Centre for Environmental Studies, Working paper 17.

(7) The tests of "compatibility" could be conducted in various ways. There is, first of all, logical incompatibility, such as two land-uses occurring in the same area of land. There are other, less stringent tests such as whether any strategy violates any accepted standard such as maximum walking distance to shops, maximum road capacities, etc.

(8) Morris Hill, "A goals achievement matrix for evaluating alternative plans", *Journal of the American Institute of Planners*, January 1968, pp. 19-29.

(9) K. W. Deutsch, "The nerves of government", New York, London 1966, talks of power in the same way as the currency of politics though influence is probably a broader concept.

(10) The list comprised the County Council, the Urban District Council, preservationists, industrialists, Trade Union Council, Sports Clubs Association, Tenants Association, farmers, landowners, motorists, the Chamber of Trade, etc. See figure 3.

(11) We did include improvements to the "game" at a later stage so that, for example, the participants representing interest-groups could raise issues of their own, though at the expense of some of their "votes", that is, of some of

their political influence.

(12) A. Etzioni, *op. cit.*

(13) To my dismay, it was accepted in full — though not without discussion — despite my having set time aside for recycling of the plan back into the evaluation procedure.

(14) Department of Town Planning, Oxford Polytechnic, Graduate Course in Urban Planning: "Year Two, Report on the Urban Plan Project", September-December 1970.

(15) See J. K. Friend's reply to Peter Hall concerning "Analysis of Interconnected Decisions Areas", *New Society*, 3 December 1970.

Action Space Analysis (with an Appendix:
The East Oxford Case Study)

The rational planning process aims at identifying the best course of action open to a decision maker.[1] One of the most concise descriptions of the rational planning process as provided by Banfield (1959) therefore includes the following three steps: "(a) the decision-maker lists all the opportunities for action open to him; (b) he identifies all the consequences which would follow from the adoption of each of the possible actions; and (c) selects the action which would be followed by the preferred set of consequences."[2]

In whichever form, the rational planning process always includes these three operations. Criticisms of rational-comprehensive planning[3] equally focus on the inability of planners to follow these prescriptions. It is argued that a "comprehensive" evaluation of all alternatives, i.e. evaluation against all consequences for the attainment of all ends, is beyond any human decision-maker.

Nevertheless, planners have attempted to follow the prescriptions of rational planning in the past. They are vindicated by Etzioni's formulation of a "mixed-scanning" strategy as a feasible approach which takes account of existing limitations of human information-handling capacity (Etzioni, 1968a,b). But, thus far, efforts to put the requirements of rational planning into practice have mainly concentrated on techniques of *evaluation* to the neglect of systematic approaches to the identification of courses of action open to decision-takers. It seems, however, obvious that even the most sophisticated evaluation technique cannot guarantee that

[1] In this paper I am setting aside the question of whether rationality in planning is an ideal worth striving for.

[2] In an earlier version, Banfield refers to some of the social science literature where this concept of the rational planning process originated. See Meyerson and Banfield (1955).

[3] For further references see Faludi (1973a,b).

the best course of action will be identified, if that course of action has not been included in the list of alternatives in the first instance. A systematic approach to the *generation* of alternatives therefore becomes a most important prerequisite of the rationality of choice. Ideally, such an approach aims at identifying *all* actions open to a decision-taker, so that they may go forward to evaluation.

Two approaches are known which have been designed with this criterion in mind: *morphological analysis* and *Analysis of Interconnected Decision Areas* (AIDA). I have reported on the use of morphological analysis in an educational project aimed at teaching the essentials of the rational planning process before (Faludi, 1972). In the case study in the appendix, examples are found of the application of AIDA in a similar context. The purpose of this paper is to highlight an improvement to both these approaches which may go beyond what has been practiced so far. This improvement is to group alternatives according to their *feasibility*.[4] The advantage of this is that fewer alternatives go forward for evaluation. The obvious objection that this limits the rationality of choice will be dealt with in the final part of this paper.

The Action Space

As a preliminary, I shall define a set of terms in which to describe both morphological analysis and AIDA. This set starts from Banfield's identification of the first step of the planning process as quoted above: "The decision-maker lists all the opportunities for action open to him. . .". This step conceives of a decision-maker and a set of possible actions which relate specifically to him as the actor. The set forms what I shall describe as the decision-maker's (multi-dimensional) *action space* (Scharpf, 1971, Friedmann, 1966/7). Within this, the decision-maker can vary his actions along a number of *dimensions*. Morphological analysis refers to these dimensions as parameters and AIDA as decision areas. The possible choices along each of these dimensions are described as parametric states and as

---

[4]In this paper, I shall talk about feasibility as expressed in degrees of probability of some programme, or part of a programme, being implemented. The meaning of "feasibility" created considerable difficulties during the project described in the appendix nevertheless, problems which have as yet not been resolved.

options by the two respective approaches. Here, these will be described as the *programme-elements* which make up the decision-maker's conceivable actions.

The problems encountered in the analysis of a decision-maker's action space may now be described as follow:

(a) The identification of the *dimensions of his action space*;
(b) The identification of the extreme points along each of these dimensions marking the *limits of the action space*;
(c) The *identification of programme elements* within these limits;
(d) The *formulation of feasible programmes* for action through combination of one programme element each from each of the dimensions of the decision-maker's action space, but paying regard to any incompatibilities between pairs of programme elements in the resulting sets.

The improvements of morphological analysis and AIDA relate to items (b) and (d) above — i.e. to the identification of the *limits of the decision-maker's action space* and to that of any *incompatibilities* between pairs of programme-elements.

The Limits of the Action Space

The improvements to be discussed originated in the application of one of the two approaches to action space analysis, morphological analysis, in an educational project. There, one of the dimensions of choice was that of how to accommodate an East-West traffic flow. In the particular case, plans existed for a by-pass. This by-pass could go either North or South of the town which seemed to exhaust the possibilities as far as the provision of a by-pass was concerned.[5] But, clearly, other solutions existed, even though they appeared unreasonable from the start, such as building a fly-over over the town centre, or a tunnel under it, instead of a by-pass. The group concerned excluded such fancy solutions on pragmatic grounds, but this left a nagging feeling of limiting the rationality of choice by restricting the range of alternatives to more conventional and obvious

[5] In the actual project, the issue was more complex because we treated traffic as a whole, and not just the East-West flow, as a parameter. However, the location of the by-pass dominated our considerations.

ones. Case studies would no doubt show that it is sometimes a technically rather elaborate solution like a tunnel which gains acceptance, its costs notwithstanding, because it avoids damages to the environment which a conventional solution would entail.[6] The problem is one of uncertainty about the limits of the action space.

One way out would obviously be that of including every conceivable possibility such as fly-overs and tunnels as solutions even to trivial traffic problems. There are two objections to this:

(1) The line must be drawn somewhere: instead of building a fly-over or a tunnel, one might load cars onto railways and ferry them around the town; one might stop cars from going through the town altogether or one could plough a four-lane motorway through the town centre thereby destroying it altogether. There is no *prima facie* reason why these solutions should be excluded apart from the fact that they seem even more unreasonable so that nobody would seriously suggest implementing them.

(2) With this systematic approach to generating all alternatives one must always beware of ending up with too many alternatives for evaluation.

The solution advocated is to note way-out possibilities and to make the intuitive judgements concerning their feasibility explicit by attaching degrees of probability of execution to them which reflect these judgements. If this is done for all programme elements (as it was in the example described in the case study), then what one gets are alternative programmes consisting of sets of programme elements, each having an aggregate probability factor attached to it which is the product of the probabilities of each one element being implemented. Alternatives may now be ranked according to these aggregate probabilities. Evaluation can start with the most feasible (highest probability) group and work down until a programme is identified which is acceptable against whichever criterion one wishes to impose.

If the more obvious solutions are unacceptable, then this approach has the advantage of providing a full record of all solutions which have been

---

[6]At least this is the result of three case studies which are only available in German. See Faludi (1970/1). For part of one of these case studies see Faludi (1973b). The final essay in this volume makes extensive use of same study.

thought of at any time during the planning process (even the fancy solutions which practical men would not have considered much further). The method thus provides a large reservoir of alternatives to draw from without necessarily assuming that all these alternatives would be evaluated at all cost. (Since the group concerned had worked out a computer programme for generating alternatives and for ranking them according to feasibility, the actual handling, even of a large number of alternatives, posed no particular problem.)

An objection against this which has been raised by Snack (1973) is that the probability of two or more programme elements being implemented in combination is not necessarily the product of the probabilities of each one being chosen. In other words, two or more low-probability solutions to two or more sub-problems might in combination give a highly feasible solution to the overall problem. This seems to go to the heart of the type of approach which morphological analysis and AIDA represent which is based on the assumption that the whole problem and its solution can be broken down into component elements, and that it is meaningful to discuss solutions in terms of these component elements and the linkages between them. The answer to Snack's objection must therefore be found in the area of linkages between programme elements. This relates back to problem (d) above, i.e. that of formulating feasible programmes of action out of the programme elements enumerated earlier.

Linkages

So far, the two methods of action space analysis have dealt with the problem of linkages between programme elements only in a relatively crude manner. Both exclude incompatible combinations, i.e. pairs of programme elements where the implementation of one programme element excludes that of the other. AIDA also makes the distinction between logical "option bars" (the AIDA term for incompatibility) and so-called policy bars and introduces a kind of contingent bar which can be removed at will. In yet further applications, costs have been attached to linkages (Hickling, 1973).

The approach suggested here is that of attaching probability factors to linkages much in the same way as to programme elements. These are again derived from one's judgement about the feasibility of programme elements being combined. The overall probability of a programme being implemented is then again the product of all probability factors attached to all the individual elements of that programme, the linkages amongst them. This gives a much more elaborate basis for the overall assessment of the feasibility of programmes. The example given is based on this approach.

It seems that there is an answer even to Snack's objection related to the assessment of feasibility of linkages (but one which has not been used in the example on which this paper is based). This is to give "bonus points" in those cases where two programme elements seem to form a particularly interesting combination making their otherwise doubtful implementation seem worthwhile. In formal terms this would sometimes mean attaching more than 100% probability to some linkages which may seem paradoxical. However, in the experience of the group, probabilities seemed notional in any case. They were a device for ranking alternatives in some convenient way relating to their feasibility, but in no way did they express the actual probability of a programme going forward for implementation.

Focussing as a Planning Strategy

The theoretical justification for the approach described is that it constitutes a planning strategy which one could describe as *focussing*. Before explaining this, a word is needed about planning strategies as an answer to the perennial problem in planning practice, *information-overload.*[7] The basic proposition is that the various criticisms of rational-comprehensive planning claiming that its requirements go beyond what human decision-makers can do are valid: decision-makers can simply not handle the amount of information required for evaluating all the alternatives open to them. Etzioni (1968a,b) has suggested mixed-scanning as one response to this situation. The approach discussed above is similar in accepting that comprehensive analysis of the total action space is impossible. But instead of Etzioni's suggestion of identifying the sector of the action-space within which a solution must be sought by a quick and by

[7]For further discussion see Faludi (1973b).

necessity superficial scan, it structures the total action space into concentric zones of feasibility. The search for a solution to the overall problem will obviously start in the zone of highest feasibility and only gradually work down into zones of lower feasibility. Figuratively speaking one might describe the first zone as the core of the action space. It tends to be that which is relatively well-perceived. The edges of the action space on the other hand are fuzzy which seems to conform to real-life when it is easy to say what can be done and much more difficult to identify the impossible.

So the theoretical justification for the approach discussed is the same as that for mixed-scanning: by accepting the limitations on human information-handling capacity as one of the facts of a situation to be reckoned with, it enables the decision-maker to handle choices in an intelligent manner, making assumptions explicit and taking decisions on the basis of the best available evidence. As with anything human, it is not an infallible method. But then, risk is a poor argument for taking no decisions at all!

References

BANFIELD, E. C. (1959) Ends and means in planning, in: *A Reader in Planning Theory* (edited by A. Faludi), Pergamon, Oxford, 1973.

ETZIONI, A. (1968a) Mixed-scanning: a "third" approach to decision-making, in: *A Reader in Planning Theory* (edited by A. Faludi), Pergamon, Oxford, 1973.

ETZIONI, A. (1968b) *The Active Society*, Collier-Macmillan, London.

FALUDI, A. (1970/1) Pluralismus im Planungsprozess, *Informationen der Arbeitsgemeinschaft für Interdisziplinäre angewandte Sozialforschung*, Vol. 2, S.75-93.

FALUDI, A. (1972) Teaching the planning process, *Journal of the Royal Town Planning Institute*, Vol. 58, pp. 111-4 (reprinted in this volume).

FALUDI, A. (1973a) *A Reader in Planning Theory*, Pergamon, Oxford.

FALUDI, A. (1973b) *Planning Theory*, Pergamon, Oxford.

FRIEDMANN, J. (1966/7) Planning as a vocation, *Plan Canada*, Vol. 6, pp. 99-124, Vol. 7, pp. 8-26.

HICKLING, A. (1973) Lecture given at the Department of Town Planning, Oxford Polytechnic, Oxford.

MEYERSON, M. and BANFIELD, E. C. (1955) *Politics, Planning and the Public Interest*, The Free Press, Glencoe.

SCHARPF, F. W. (1971) Komplexität als Schranke der politischen Planung, Paper presented to the AGM of the German Political Science Association, Mannheim.

SNACK, R. (1973) Private Communication.

Appendix:
The East Oxford Case Study *

Introduction

This report is concerned with an attempt to apply some of the new systematic processes of plan generation to a complex urban situation.

Our action space was defined by the assumption that we had been asked by the Oxford City Council to advise them on the future development of East Oxford. Information about the present situation in the area was obtained chiefly from the document published by the City Council ("East Oxford Plan: interim report"). We had some background information from seminars and game situations. In this, an educational context, we did not devote valuable time and effort to collecting information, because we were concerned with developing a method. Of course, in a real planning situation, the results of the method will only be as good as the input information.

Framework and General Objectives

Generating a plan involves making a number of interrelated decisions. These decisions are concerned with selecting the best solutions to the problems of the area planned.

In complex situations solutions to different problems may conflict with each other. For example, if one has a housing shortage, one solution to this problem — to build more houses — will affect other problems such as parking, traffic flow, and so on. Again a decision to build a school at plot X will conflict with a decision to allow light industry on plot X.

Thus it is vital that the implications of interrelationships between

*The group comprised the following students of the first year of the Graduate Diploma Course in Urban Planning at Oxford Polytechnic: A. Lachlan, A. Maclean, J. Obscuro-Lango, I. Rae, R. Reade and L. Thorn. The project was conducted in 1972/3 as part of a larger project comparing approaches to plan generation. It was supervised by Mrs. Sue Batty and the author.

decisions should be clearly recognised and understood during the plan generation process. The process of plan generation implies that one should be able to decide which set of solutions (strategy) is superior to all others on defined criteria. Now it is obvious that one cannot select the "best" set if this is not included in the strategies considered. So a second vital characteristic of any satisfactory planning process is that a wide range of possible alternatives should be systematically generated for evaluation and selection.

We felt that these two requirements — the ability to make explicit interrelationships between decisions, and the possibility of systematically generating a wide range of alternatives — were met by the AIDA approach (Analysis of Interconnected Decision Areas).

The AIDA Approach

The most fundamental decisions in any plan generation process are those that affect, or are affected by, other decisions. The AIDA approach allows one to identify these fundamental areas of decision, and to generate all the possible alternative strategies resulting from different combinations of decisions within these decision areas. This will become clearer as we describe the application of the process to the East Oxford situation.

Identification of Decision Areas

Our first task was to define our context, and identify the fundamental areas for decision. In practice we did not spend much time on the first point, but merely assumed different aspects of the context as the questions arose. For example we decided, quite arbitrarily, to assume that the City Council had told us that the Eastwyke Farm Road Plan had been dropped. (In a real planning situation the planners would continually refer back to their clients for guidance on context.) The next step — the definition of fundamental decision areas — was more of a problem. Group discussion* revealed that there are a variety of different ways of defining

*Throughout the project we used a kind of "Delphi" approach whereby if we had anything to decide each member of the group would go away and make an individual decision, and then we would meet and "hammer out" a group decision where individual decisions differed.

these decisions. Eventually we decided to generate decision areas from the problems of East Oxford. We defined twelve major problems that we thought would be related to fundamental decisions:

(1) Housing shortage;
(2) Disrepair, decay, delapidation of buildings;
(3) Lack of facilities for indoor recreation/entertainment;
(4) Need for new Middle School;
(5) Possible need for further schools;
(6) Possible need for more shops;
(7) Traffic congestion;
(8) Unsightly derelict land;
(9) Pressure on parking;
(10) Lack of public open space;
(11) Conflicts between industry and residential areas;
(12) Conflicts between through traffic and pedestrians.

Definition of Options within Decision Areas

The next step was to explore possible responses to the problems we had defined. For example given a possible need for further schools one might (1) do nothing about the problem until an obvious need arises, (2) reserve land for one further school, (3) reserve land for two further schools. These, then, are our *options* within this decision area (see Table 1).

In defining options we met with a number of difficulties. The first, which we had encountered before when discussing decision areas, was that we were uncertain about the level of detail that we should be considering at this stage. Should we be working in terms of general policies, or specific plans defined in spatial terms? We decided eventually that we would have to go through at least one "round" of the AIDA method at a very general level, selecting some general strategy or strategies that we could then use as a context for a second round at a more detailed level of description.

A second problem was that in many decision areas the number of possible options are almost limitless, as one can produce many possible combinations of different solutions. To reduce our options to a manageable number we had to group options into "packages" representative of particular kinds of solutions. For example in the decision

TABLE 1 Initial Set of Decision Areas and Options

	Decision areas		Options
(1)	Housing shortage	1.1	Redevelopment
		1.2	Build on derelict sites
		1.3	Some derelict, some conversion
		1.4	Conversion
(2)	Shortage of public open space	2.1	Do nothing
		2.2	Street Landscape
		2.3	Change of land use
(3)	Disrepair, decay, delapidation	3.1	Do nothing
		3.2	Emphasis on redevelopment
		3.3	Emphasis on GIA
(4)	Lack of indoor recreation facility	4.1	No change
		4.2	Intensify use of existent facility
		4.3	Change of build. Use or redevelop
(5)	New Middle School site	5.1	Decide on site (10 options)
(6)	Need for further schools	6.1	Do nothing
		6.2	Reserve one plot
		6.3	Reserve two plots
(7)	Shops	7.1	Do nothing
		7.2	Improve existing
		7.3	Sites for new shops
(8)	Traffic congestion	8.1	Do nothing
		8.2	City level strategy
		8.3	Restrain traffic on Cowley
		8.4	Through traffic only in Radials
(9)	Unsightly derelict land	9.1	Do nothing
		9.2	Landscape
		9.3	Build
(10)	Parking	10.1	Do nothing
		10.2	Full parking policy
		10.3	Some parking
		10.4	Parking only for residents
(11)	Conflict Industry-Housing	11.1	Move all industry out
		11.2	Rezone industry (permissive)
		11.3	Move industry between housing (compulsory)
		11.4	Do nothing

area arising from the housing shortage there was a package with an emphasis on redevelopment, and a package with an emphasis on conversion. Each option could include minority elements from other options. In other words the options were policy guide lines rather than rigid implementation procedures.

Discovering Option Bars

We now had 11 decision areas* each with several options. The next step was to investigate the relationships between different options, and define "option bars" where an option in one decision area conflicts with an option in another decision area. Option bars could arise through policy

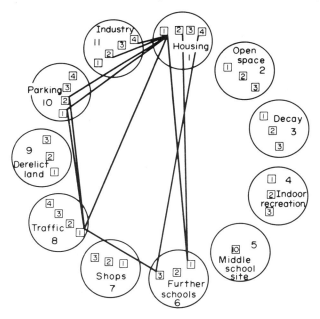

Fig. 1   Initial Set of Decision Areas and Option Bars.

*The two traffic decision areas had been collapsed into one because they had generated similar options.

considerations or physical considerations. For example the option of leaving industry alone and the option of building houses on industrial sites is physically impossible, while the option of building more housing is politically incompatible with the option of not reserving land for schools.

Once the option bars were established the pattern of linkages between all the decisions could be assessed. Six decision areas (including shopping, indoor recreation, decay) had no option that conflicted with options in other decision areas at this general level of analysis (Fig. 1).

These decision areas were therefore set aside to be considered later in the plan generation process. This left five areas, and nineteen options, from which 388 alternative strategies were generated, with the aid of our computer program (Table 2 and Figs. 2 and 3).

TABLE 2 Set of Decision Areas and Options Investigated
on Strategic Level

	Decision areas		Options
(1)	Traffic congestion	1.1	Do nothing
		1.2	City level strategy
		1.3	Restrain traffic on Cowley
		1.4	Through traffic only in 3 radials
(2)	Parking	2.1	Do nothing
		2.2	Full parking policy
		2.3	Provide some parking
		2.4	Parking only for residents
(3)	Housing	3.1	Redevelopment
		3.2	Build on derelict sites
		3.3	Some derelict, some conversion
		3.4	Conversion
(4)	Housing-Industry conflict	4.1	Move all industry out
		4.2	Rezone industry (permissive)
		4.3	Move all industry in between housing (compulsory)
		4.4	Do nothing
(5)	Further schools	5.1	Do nothing
		5.2	Reserve one plot
		5.3	Reserve two plots

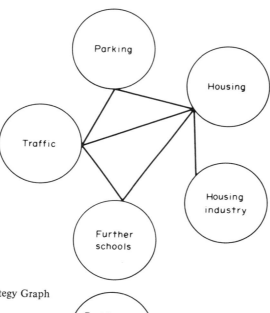

Fig. 2   Strategy Graph

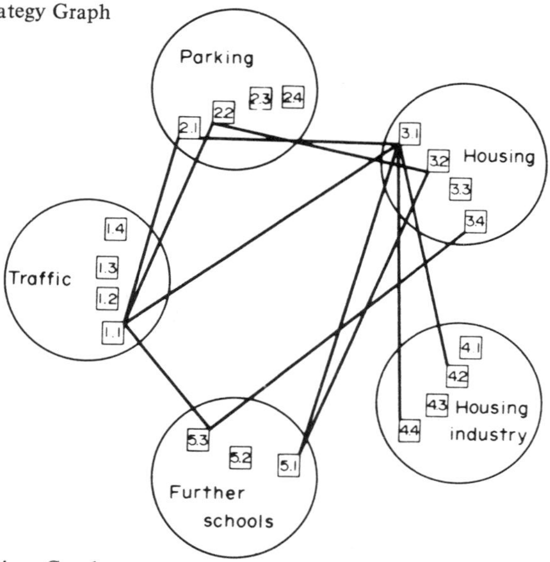

Fig. 3   Options Graph

Selection of a General Strategy

At this stage we had before us 388 alternative strategies for the area. Our next problem was to select a strategy or strategies, that would be worth considering in more detail in the "second round". We wanted to develop a systematic selection process where the criteria for selection could be "switched in" to suit different requirements, being as separate as possible from the actual method of selection.

There are two important considerations when choosing any plan: (1) is it the "best" plan in terms of the distribution of costs and benefits, and (2) will the plan be accepted and implemented by the client? These are quite separate questions, and our selection method treats them separately.

Acceptability to the Users of East Oxford

This part of the evaluation takes into account the different effects that different decision options will have on the users of East Oxford. Every option was given a separate score (on a scale from 1 to 5) for each of four criteria:

(1) Costs (financial or otherwise) suffered by any users as a result of the option;
(2) Benefits to any users;
(3) The professional judgement of the planning team;
(4) The attitude of local pressure groups.

These four scores were taken to be four independent estimates of the acceptability of the options to the users of East Oxford (see Table 3). These particular criteria have, no doubt, many faults, but we would like to emphasise the way in which we used these scores rather than the actual criteria we fed into the process. Most evaluation methods involve adding weighted scores on different criteria and obtaining a single aggregate score for each strategy. We feel that this is unsatisfactory because (a) one cannot assume that scores from different criteria can be added linearly, and (b) the process of weighting criteria is a difficult and arbitrary process that is best avoided. For these reasons we turned to the technique known as *dominance analysis*. Obviously any strategy that has a poorer score on all four criteria than another strategy can be rejected whatever the weighting system. Dominance analysis simple identifies that *"nondominant"*

TABLE 3 Acceptability Matrix

Options		Criteria			
		Political informal	Planner opinion	Benefits to users	Costs to users
1.1	Do nothing	2	2	1	1
1.2	Restrain traffic on Cowley	4	3	3	3
1.3	City level strategy	4	2	4	3
1.4	Through traffic only on R	4	4	4	4
2.1	Do nothing	1	2	1	2
2.2	Full parking policy	5	2	2	2
2.3	Provide some parking	4	4	4	4
2.4	Park only for residents	4	4	4	4
3.1	Redevelopment	2	4	3	5
3.2	Build on derelict sites	4	4	5	4
3.3	Some derelict, some conversion	4	4	3	4
3.4	Conversion	3	5	3	4
4.1	Move all industry out	4	3	3	4
4.2	Rezone industry	4	3	2	3
4.3	Move inbetween housing industry	4	4	4	4
4.4	Do nothing	2	2	1	1
5.1	Do nothing	2	3	1	2
5.2	Reserve one plot	3	3	4	4
5.3	Reserve two plots	4	4	4	4

Criteria	(1) Attitude of local pressure groups
	(2) Planners' value judgement
	(3) Benefits to all users
	(4) Costs to all users
Values	1 to 5 (3 neutral)

solutions that can be rejected, leaving the *dominant* ones for further consideration.

Feasibility

Our aim was to produce a strategy which had a reasonable chance of being implemented. We therefore built into our selection process a feasibility assessment. (Feasibility here includes financial, political, and physical feasibility.) First we gave each option a score (from 1 to 5) based on the probability that this option, if proposed, would be implemented. We then adjusted our score according to the certainty of our judgements using the conversion table below (Table 4). This resulted in the feasibilities given in Table 5.

TABLE 4 Table used in adjusting feasibility assessment to certainty
with which judgements were held (adapted from: B. M. Köhler,
Verfahren der Bewertung, in: Arbeitsberichte zur
Planungsmethodik, Vol. 1, Stuttgart, 1969)

	Completely feasible	Very feasible	Neutral	Very unfeasible	Completely unfeasible
Very certain	100	70	50	30	0
Certain	85	65	50	35	15
Uncertain	70	60	50	40	30

Criteria (1) Political
          (2) Financial
          (3) Physical

TABLE 5 Feasibility of Options

1.1	Do nothing	50
1.2	Restrain traffic on Cowley	50
1.3	City level strategy	40
1.4	Through traffic only on R	85
2.1	Do nothing	50
2.2	Full parking policy	35
2.3	Provide some parking	85
2.4	Park only for residents	60
3.1	Redevelopment	50
3.2	Build on derelict sites	85
3.3	Some derelict some conversion	100
3.4	Conversion	85
4.1	Move all industry out	15
4.2	Rezone industry	100
4.3	Move inbetween housing industry	65
4.4	Do nothing	40
5.1	Do nothing	85
5.2	Reserve one plot	40
5.3	Reserve two plots	30

TABLE 6 Feasibility of links between options.
(For the designations of options see the previous figures)

	1.1	1.2	1.3	1.4	2.1	2.2	2.3	2.4	3.1	3.2	3.3	3.4	4.1	4.2	4.3	4.4	5.1	5.2	5.3
1.1																			
1.2	0																		
1.3	0	0																	
1.4	0	0	0																
2.1	0	40	15	35															
2.2	0	50	30	60	0														
2.3	65	60	65	65	0	0													
2.4	30	70	40	85	0	0	0												
3.1	0	60	70	50	0	50	70	85											
3.2	60	70	70	60	50	60	70	85	0										
3.3	70	70	70	70	60	65	85	85	0	0									
3.4	85	85	70	70	85	65	0	85	0	0	0								
4.1	100	70	85	85	85	85	100	85	0	70	85	85							
4.2	60	70	50	50	85	85	100	70	50	85	85	85	0						
4.3	85	60	60	65	85	85	100	85	0	70	85	85	0	0					
4.4	50	100	70	35	70	85	70	60	0	60	85	85	0	0	0				
5.1	100	100	100	85	85	85	70	85	0	0	35	70	85	85	85	85			
5.2	60	70	70	60	70	70	60	70	85	60	85	60	85	75	75	70	0		
5.3	0	70	70	50	60	70	60	70	70	50	85	0	85	75	75	70	0	0	

We could have measured the probability of implementation of each strategy simply by multiplying together the probabilities of each option in the strategy. However, this does not take into account the case where two options are very feasible, considered singly, but their combination is not very feasible. (For example, two high-cost options might each be within the City's budget when taken singly, but a plan that included the combination of both projects might be virtually certain of rejection on financial grounds.) We therefore included scores for the feasibility of links between options (Table 6). The overall feasibility score for a strategy was taken to be the geometric mean of the feasibility scores for (a) each option in the strategy, (b) each option link in the strategy.

Selection Based on Acceptability and Feasibility

We now had a list of dominant strategies, and a list of feasibility scores for every strategy. The most satisfactory way to proceed from here would have been to take the dominant strategies which were above a certain level of feasibility and then apply a more refined selection method to the selected set. There are several possibilities here. We might have tried to group the selected strategies into types and choose one strategy that typified each type. Or we might have used different acceptability criteria and gone through the selection process again. We could have considered the frequency of different options within the selected set, and found the most "robust" strategy, whose options occurred most frequently.

In fact, we found that we did not have time to follow up any of these possibilities. Our project timetable forced us to choose a strategy as quickly as possible, so that we would have time to consider detailed alternatives, and come up with some sort of physical plan. So we took a short-cut, and ranked each of the top feasibility and acceptability scores and chose the strategy that had the highest average rank (Table 7). Of course, this could not be recommended in any real planning situation, for one is not justified in assuming that a feasibility rank is as important as an acceptability rank.

TABLE 7 Identification of Preferred Strategy

Strategy no.	Feasibility	Acceptability				Options				
353		17	20	16	18	1.4	2.3	3.4	4.3	5.1
385		17	20	16	18	1.4	2.4	3.4	4.3	5.1
344	h	19	19	20	20	1.4	2.3	3.3	4.3	5.2
376	i	19	19	19	20	1.4	2.4	3.3	4.3	5.2
342	g	20	19	17	19	1.4	2.3	3.3	4.2	5.3
110	h	20	18	16	18	1.2	2.3	3.3	4.2	5.3
354		18	20	19	20	1.4	2.3	3.4	4.3	5.2
386		18	20	19	20	1.4	2.4	3.4	4.3	5.2
345		20	20	19	20	1.4	2.3	3.3	4.3	5.3
377		20	20	19	20	1.4	2.4	3.3	4.3	5.3
374	l	29	19	17	19	1.4	2.4	3.3	4.2	5.3
365	o	19	19	21	20	1.4	2.4	3.2	4.3	5.2
334	w	20	20	21	20	1.4	2.3	3.2	4.3	5.3
250		20	18	21	19	1.3	2.4	3.2	4.3	4.3
330		20	19	20	20	1.4	2.3	3.2	4.1	5.3
360		20	20	21	20	1.4	2.4	3.2	4.3	5.3
362		20	19	20	20	1.4	2.4	3.2	4.1	5.3
Dominant options:						1.4	2.3	3.4	4.3	5.1
							2.4	3.3		5.3
								3.2		(5.2)

Preferred strategy: 1.4 Restrain through traffic to 3 radials
2.3 Provide some parking: 1 car park, restrain on street
3.3 Housing: build on some derelict, some conversion
4.3 Move all industry in between housing: compulsory
5.3 Reserve 2 plots for further schools

Arriving at a More Detailed Strategy

The general strategy selected by the group was used as the basis for a second round of the AIDA method. The opportunity to go through repeated rounds at more and more detailed levels of description is an important feature of the approach. Different methods of defining decision areas, different kinds of option bars, and different criteria for selecting strategies, can be applied to suit different levels of analysis.

In this second round the previous, general, context had been in effect further defined by deciding on our general strategy. In addition to these five decided policies we also had a number of problems left over from the first round (indoor recreation, disrepair, etc.) which we could now take into account.

At this more detailed level of description we found that decision areas could be defined in terms of plots of land, because in the particular case of East Oxford the number of places where change was envisaged led to a manageable number of decisions. This presented us with an opportunity to define decision areas in spatial terms, in contrast to the non-spatial viewpoint of the first round.

We considered each plot (decision area) in turn and considered the possible land-uses for which it might be suitable, taking into account our general policies, and the problems we had defined. Each land-use became an option. Some plots seemed to have only one obvious land-use, and these dropped out of the process. We then defined option bars, as in the

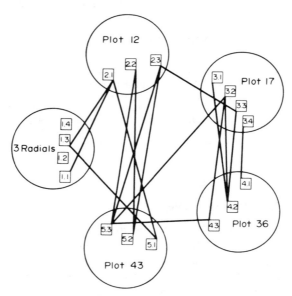

Fig. 4   Option Graph for Detailed Level.

previous round. There were more bars this time, because obvious physical incompatibilities were evident at this level, e.g. if one has decided to build one car park, a car park on one plot is incompatible with a car park on another plot. The list of decision areas, options, and option bars at this level is illustrated (Table 8, Fig. 4).

There are two decision areas unrelated to plots. These are the decisions concerned with traffic and parking, which relate to the general policies chosen from the previous round.

A preferred strategy was selected in the same way as before, with one

TABLE 8 Decision Areas and Options on a More Detailed Level

	Decision areas		Options
(1)	Through traffic in radials only	1.1	Link at Howard & Magdalen Road
		1.2	Link at Marston and Rectory Road
		1.3	Ring Road as link
		1.4	Both links (1.1 & 1.2)
(2)	Plot 12	2.1	Car park
		2.2	Housing
		2.3	Open Space
(3)	Plot 17	3.1	Housing
		3.2	Indoor Recreation
		3.3	Open Space
		3.4	School
(4)	Plot 36	4.1	Two Schools
		4.2	Housing
		4.3	1 School and Indoor Recreation
(5)	Plot 43	5.1	Parking
		5.2	Housing
		5.3	Indoor Recreation

Single policy decisions

(6) Reduce on street parking in radials

(7) Plot 22. For Open Space

(8) Plot 28 For Housing or Residents' Car Park

(9) ½ Plot for Housing

exception. The group felt that the criteria for "acceptability" would need to be different in this round. Detailed proposals may be generally acceptable in East Oxford but may be unacceptable to a minority — specifically, those directly affected by the proposals. For this reason, the acceptability criteria used at this level were:

(1) Effect on people in the immediate vicinity;
(2) Value as assessed by the planning team;
(3) Costs (financial and other) to users;
(4) Benefits to users.

The results are shown in Table 9.

TABLE 9 Acceptability Assessment of Options on Detailed Level

		Criteria			
	Options	Residents	Planners	Social costs	Social benefits
1.1	Link at Magdalen, Howard Rds.	1	3	4	4
1.2	Link at Marston, Rectory Rds.	1	3	2	3
1.3	Do nothing	3	2	1	5
1.4	Both links (1.1, 1.2)	1	4	4	3
2.1	Car park	2	4	3	4
2.2	Housing	3	4	4	4
2.3	Open space	5	4	4	4
3.1	Housing	4	2	4	4
3.2	Indoor recreation	5	5	4	5
3.3	Open space	2	4	5	4
3.4	School	5	2	3	4
4.1	Two schools	2	3	4	4
4.2	Housing	4	3	4	5
4.3	One school and indoor recreation	3	4	4	5
5.1	Parking	4	2	2	2
5.2	Housing	4	3	4	4
5.3	Indoor recreation	3	4	4	4

Criteria: (1) Residents closely affected by decision
(2) Planners' value judgement
(3) Social costs
(4) Social benefits
Values: 1 to 5 (3 neutral)

Conclusions

The AIDA approach allows one to break down the process of generating a plan into a series of decision areas, to analyse the interrelationships between possible options, and to generate a large number of alternative solutions systematically. A preferred strategy can then be selected from these alternatives on the basis of a set of explicit criteria.

Systematising the plan generation process in this way helps the planner by providing a structure for his decision-making. It also helps the client by making clear the assumptions and criteria on which the plan is based.

There are a number of ways in which one could add to, or refine, the method we used. For example, it may often be worth going through three or more "rounds" of AIDA instead of arbitrarily defining only two levels of analysis. It may be possible, in fact, to investigate the structure of the problem *before* proceeding with an AIDA approach (Christopher Alexander's "Notes on the Synthesis of Form" may be of help here). One could then assign different decisions to different levels by a less arbitrary method.

There are many ways in which we might improve our selection technique. Having obtained our shortlist of feasible, acceptable strategies, we might have chosen the most "robust" solution, or a set of solutions representing different qualities, or we might have refined our criteria for acceptability, and chosen the "best" strategy from weighted criteria. We could have left some options open for future decision.

Perhaps one should end by making it clear what AIDA cannot do. It cannot define decision areas, options, option bars, or criteria for selection. This is the input that is fed into the method. The output, the plan, depends on this input. There is no magic formula that brings up the appropriate plan for the appropriate situation. If you faced a series of planning teams with the same physical situation, and told them to use our method, they would each arrive at a different plan.

Part III

Sociology in Planning Education, or: A Look into the Mirror

The three essays in this part arise from my continuing interest in the role of the social sciences, and in particular of sociology, in planning education. This interest, however, has always transcended the narrow question of the role of the social sciences in planning. The key-issue, as far as these papers are concerned, is the manner in which assumptions about the nature of planning itself are reflected in its relations with other disciplines right down to the thorny problems of curriculum planning and the day-to-day conduct of learning and teaching in the planning schools.

The reader will observe that these papers are partly based on empirical research. This consisted, firstly, of two postal questionnaires, sent to planning schools and to sociology lecturers and, secondly, of interviews held with about forty sociologists, some of whom had already been included in the mail survey held previously. The quotations in the first paper and most of those in the second paper are from the transcripts of these interviews. The remaining quotations and the data are drawn from the mail survey. The latter also generated information on course structure, place of sociology in the curriculum, and readings used on sociology courses, to be found in the working paper from which the second essay derives.

The essays themselves are each of a different character. As mentioned above, the second comes out of a working paper, whereas the first is an address to a seminar on *Uses of Social Science in Urban Planning*. This explains the difference in style. However, both reflect the same concern with the newly formulated generalist concept of the role of the planner and the ensuing educational policy which was the diet on which planning educators lived in those days. In this respect therefore, these papers have a close affinity with the essays in Part I. They are different, however, in that they focus on the effects, instead of the emergence, of the generalist

101

policy. But, as with the previous ones, I would like to think that they have an element of sociological argument to them, explaining the beliefs and actions of human beings partly by reference to their social situations.

In a way, the first two essays with their mutually supportive findings are heavily dated. As outlined in the third essay (details are to be found in the third essay of Part I on the changing scene of British planning education), the generalist concept has been abandoned in favour of something more akin to the generalist-with-a-specialism concept which I advocate. Also, sociologists have been welcomed in the planning world since, writing critical studies about its practice and ideology which figure prominently on reading lists of the planning schools. They now play a prominent role in discussions in the planning education field which has generally been infused with substantial awareness of the social sciences and with the critical attitudes towards society which they are bringing to bear.

However, apart from indicating the historic origin of the present situation in planning education, the first two essays also form the essential background to the last. In some instances, they foreshadow its arguments, for example, where the second paper carefully explores the idea of relatively autonomous "departments of sociology" within the larger planning schools. In some respects, they also form a contrast. They are imbued with optimism about the potential role of sociology and the social sciences. The last paper, as against this, builds on several years' experience of working in an environment where none of the constraints depicted in the first essays was very strong. The essay thus strikes a sober note: the social-science based planning theory asked for in the previous papers will have to be built from within planning itself, and will not be supplied from without. To this end, a complex course structure is sketched out which might generate the necessary dialogue, but whether sociologists, as indeed other social scientists, will show themselves willing to cooperate must remain an open question.

The Experience of Sociologists
in their Collaboration with Planners

Introduction

When talking to an audience of young planners, there appears to be no safer strategy than what I have once called planner-bashing. From my observations, the speakers who indulge in it are always those who receive the warmest and most spontaneous applause which is an interesting reflection of the frame of mind or, even more, of the basic insecurity which seems to prevail amongst younger planners in any case. With this audience, however, in which non-planners are dominant, I am in danger of provoking that traditional British reaction of coming out in the defence of the underdog. I am saying this because it might well appear that I, too, am doing a fair amount of planner-bashing, and I would therefore like to observe that my comments are derived from reactions which I got when interviewing something like 40 sociologists who had been in some form of contact with town planners. So, if you want, I am only the medium through which you receive some feedback about the way in which sociologists tend to react to the experiences to which they are exposed in the planning world.

This brings me to explain the background of my study. I am engaged in research into the role of sociology in town planning education. The idea of going out into the field and asking sociologists about their actual experiences was based on the assumption that courses in sociology given to prospective town planners should primarily aim at creating a basis on which professional collaboration between the two could, in future, perhaps become more satisfactory and avoid the pitfalls and frustrations which it may hold for both sides at present.

The respondents were in the main sociologists but included some people from related disciplines such as political science, social geography, economics and social administration. These few representatives of other social sciences whom I have interviewed more or less accidentally did not, in any significant way, differ in their reactions from the great majority of the sociologists. I think this supports the proposition which I wish to develop in this paper, namely that, to a large extent, the difficulties of collaboration result not so much from the attitudes and outlooks of the social scientists but rather from the "generalist" role-concept which the planners hold of themselves.

Interviewing sociologists about matters germane to their own discipline is a highly rewarding experience. Indeed, what I had were conversations with people of outstanding qualities and wealth of experience in this field. But sociologists, being constantly aware of values, social relationships, ideological distortions, etc., tend to give answers which are more than mere statements of fact. This is a strength and a weakness of my material at the same time because the answers are almost invariably as much statements of fact as interpretations of these facts in the light of the respondents' own theories.

This brings me to the last consideration about the nature of the material on which my work is based. These are some observations which limit the reliability of my data, and I therefore wish to preface my paper by a word of warning that none of my propositions can be taken as more than hypotheses. This is because the total population of sociologists who have been in contact with planners is unknown, and my respondents consequently do not constitute a statistical sample. Nor did the type of questions set, and the type of answers received, lend themselves very readily to quantitative analysis. This is because many of the answers included an *interpretation of facts*, and it is in the nature of an interpretation that its validity is independent of the frequency with which it is advanced. The only sort of quantitative analysis which I have therefore attempted is of the vaguest kind to indicate where the great majority of my respondents reacted in very similar ways and where thus the existence of a fairly broad consensus of opinion can be assumed.

This brings me to the structure of this paper. My analysis will be qualitative rather than numerate, and it is inevitable that it should be coloured by my own assumptions about the present nature of town planning. Thus, this paper will begin with developing the concepts of the *"generalist" planner* who holds himself fully responsible for the "planning process", and the sociologist as the *"contributor"* with all the consequences which flow from this superior-subordinate relationship. At the present stage, there is very little known about planners and their frame of mind, working conditions and professional relations with other disciplines, and this conceptual analysis may push the limits of the unknown a bit further. Beyond this I, personally, of course claim no more than having brought the experiences of many sociologists together who — and this is one of my findings — work more often than not in isolation, not so much by inclination but as a result of their inferior position in the planning world. This and other findings will eventually give me cause for some reflections.

"Value-freedom" in an Operational Context

As a preliminary, it is probably best for me to lay my cards on the table and say that I regard planning as a kind of social technology. This stands for the application of social theory to the task of rendering purposeful interventions into the working of social forces more rational. Such an application would be informed by an awareness of the nature of social theory, including the indeterminacy of most of its propositions, and sensitivity to the fact that there are value-judgements involved in planning work, if only to differing degrees and in different ways.

The idea of a social technology informed by social theory may evoke criticism from sociologists. Some are inclined to say that sociology should be value-free and that, if so, sociology could not help in making value-decisions, and *ipso facto* in planning work. Proponents of this view therefore regard the nature of sociology as a discipline as the key-variable in the professional relationship between sociologists and planners. This proposition was, however, unrelated to what I found in the field. Though in the abstract many respondents felt that value-freedom *would* constitute a limitation of the sociologist in planning, they did *not* report many actual instances in which this had happened in their own experience. This is curious and to me suggests a vague feeling on their part that value-freedom somehow *ought* to constrain them probably as a remnant of their academic training. Despite this, in their day-to-day conduct, respondents had been willing to immerse themselves in discussions of what ought to happen in a planning project.

Let me briefly elaborate on this point. My respondents, and in particular those who were engaged in practical planning work, felt on the whole that they could *not* avoid committing themselves, or indeed, that they had an *obligation* to give their personal judgements. Witness the following answers: "I am a pragmatic sort of person. Given a situation where decisions *have* to be made I accept that one can only be as objective as one can. . . ."

". . . if a decision was about to be made, then it was my *duty* to consider what I thought the right course was. . . ."

"The implicit assumption of a planner, when he asks one into his work is that you will be there not only to give him factual information, but to *commit* yourselves in terms of *value-assumptions* and *value-positions*. I think it's therefore dishonest to accept employment of this kind under any other terms."

Other respondents made a clear distinction between their own values, which they were prepared to bring into play, and the value-freedom of sociology as a discipline: "I believe that I have the responsibility for my own knowledge. I would say: 'It is *not sociology* that is telling you to do this, *but I!*' "

In this context it is pertinent to say that it was *only from academics*, i.e. sociology-lecturers in planning schools, that reports of restraints of this kind came. One other respondent, who was acting in two different contexts simultaneously, highlighted what the importance of this academic context was: "Yes, *as an academic* I feel this restraint, but as soon as one is concerned with planning, then one must accept that the best is the only way of the good. . . ."

Obviously, most writing in sociology is done by academics, and so seems to be the writing about sociology and planning. The norm of value-freedom, Gouldner argues[1] is one which has particular relevance to the academic context in that the reward-system of the academic world is geared towards perfection rather than applicability of findings. It may thus be that, as some respondents said, sociology has not developed as an operational skill, which is the equivalent of saying that there are few social technologies in the sense in which we used this term. Sociology itself, but

---

[1]A. W. Gouldner, Anti-Minotaur: The Myth of a Value-Free Sociology, in: I. L. Horowitz (Ed.) *The New Sociology* (1964) pp. 196-217.

not necessarily the form which it takes in academic departments, seems however to be well capable of informing and improving decisions of those engaged in practical work. Even though sociologists, most of the respondents had indeed adapted to an operational context and had brought their personal values into play in decision-making, at least where they had been given the chance. They had done so, however, in an explicit way, such as they had been trained to do.

Based on these findings I would say that the key-variable in the professional relationship between sociologists and planners is *not* the nature of sociology as a discipline. Indeed, my view is that planning will *only become effective*, possibly, if it develops a theory of the *very nature as sociology has*.

"Generalist" and "Contributor"

I found, against this, the position of sociologists in relation to planners, i.e. the flows of information and commands which existed between them, to constitute this key-variable. Here I observed that, only where the sociologist was in an *independent* position was it possible for him to bring his expertise to bear in such a way that he was reasonably satisfied about the usefulness of his contribution.

A number of respondents were fairly senior academics and researchers whose involvement in planning was that of consultants. In the description of their relations with planners they often observed that they had influenced, or even determined, their own terms of reference. It was noticeable that these were broad enough to allow for a general argument rather than expecting the sociologist only to provide a specific input. The ability to make certain terms of reference a pre-condition of accepting commissions is clearly an important asset. It probably stems from the fact that skills in social research are still a scarce resource.

But, only a few enjoy this privilege, and for the majority of sociologists, in particular for those in more junior positions, there is, in the words of one respondent "just a lot of wilderness". It is this ideal-type of the junior isolated sociologist, tucked away in the back-room of a local authority planning department that I want to develop for you as a complement to the ideal-type of the generalist planner.

For a definition of the "generalist" concept I can do no better than quote an official statement of the TPI: "Town Planning is a process, involving a recurring cycle of operations, for preparing and controlling the implementation of plans for changing systems of land-use and settlement of varying scale. In this activity the chartered planner plays the *central and crucial professional rôle*. His special skill, a *command of the planning process as a whole*, qualifies and entitles him to organise and co-ordinate all planning operations as well as to design and control the implementation of the plan or policy."[2]

The complementary idea of "contributory skills" is also to be found in a Council Statement of the TPI: "However many contributors are called on, the planner must retain his *central rôle* of organising, directing and synthesising in the planning process. The professional responsibility cannot be shifted from him, nor eliminated, without grave consequences for planning, and indeed for the human environment. In the planning team, therefore *the contributors should be responsible to him....*"[3]

This, to me, suggests that the "generalist" planner does not wish to see the "contributors" contribute in such a way that they would inform his decisions. The role accorded to the contributor is rather an *instrumental* one, i.e. he ought to restrict himself to providing those *inputs* which the planner has specified for him. One may also observe that sociologists are lumped together with a whole range of other disciplines as if the nature of their contribution was in a way the same as that of, for argument's sake, the surveyors. This appears to be very much in the nature of what planners perceive the "social inputs" into their plans to be. One respondent for instance reported having been told by a planner: "I would like an answer from the sociologist which enables me to look up what people want . . . in the same way as I can look up plot-ratios. . . ."

Lastly it is pertinent to refer to a statement by Professor Kantorowich, who has been instrumental in developing the "generalist" concept and who defined the area in which he wanted to see the planner dominating as that of "the planner's office". This underlines that this whole question

[2]The Town Planning Institute, Revised Scheme for the Final Examination, Progress Report on Membership Policy, March 1967.

[3]The Town Planning Institute, *The Relationship of the Disciplines which Contribute in Town and Country Planning*, Council Statement of 29th March 1967.

originated in a territorial dispute, a question of recognised boundaries and of mutual respect of professional integrity amongst different skill-groups engaged in local authority technical services. Very crudely speaking, what this means, and this must be understood against the history of the "generalist" vs. "specialist" conflict which has raged in the TPI in the early and mid-sixties, is that local authority planners want to be accepted and respected as equals amongst equals by their peers in local authority bureaucracies. These peers are however essentially other *technical* professionals such as architects, engineers and surveyors. The sociologists are not a party to this dispute, at least not up until now.

About this concept of the planner as a generalist and the corollary idea of "contributory" skills the following observations can be made:

(1) It is ideological in the sense of reflecting *tangible interests* of a significant part of the membership of the TPI. What is at stake are, in the main, promotion chances, including promotions to chief officer grade. This fact, which in itself of course does not invalidate it, warrants some suspicion nevertheless.

(2) The second observation which one can make about the "generalist" concept is that it *is not generalist at all*. It can be interpreted as part and parcel of the on-going process of specialisation and differentiation of public bureaucracies. An indication for this is the fact that planners tend to emphasise the role of statutory procedures of planning as constituting the basis of *their specialism*. This was perceived very clearly by my respondents, either directly by observing this to constitute the special skill of planners, or indirectly by stating that this "mystery of the process" was that part of planning operations which they did *not* understand. As one respondent qualified in both planning and sociology and thus perhaps not too unsympathetic to planners said: "Development control might be the *one area* where planners are *real specialists*. It is the one field of planning where they can blind you."

That nothing like a claim for a generalism in the sense of a comprehensive guidance of the social system, or even some modest co-ordination of government activities is involved in the "generalist" concept is also clear from the following of Professor Kantorowich's statements: "I claim no Superman omniscience and omnipotence for the planner. He is expert *only in his own field*, but this requires him to be sufficiently well-informed around it to be able to communicate and interact regularly and effectively with experts in related disciplines."[4]

(3) My final observation is about the nature of town planning, again as reflected in a paper by Professor Kantorowich. He compared planning with "creative" skills such as those of musicians, poets, artists and architects. These, to me, appear to be of quite a different kind than the discipline of sociology — or indeed any other of the social sciences — require. They take a predominantly intuitive approach to synthesising experiences into an overall solution. Such a synthesis is almost inevitably the work of individuals. This approach is certainly in contradiction to the idea of team work and, incidentally, also to consumer-participation, thus leading to the idealism and paternalism of planners which were the object of many observations made by my respondents. You will therefore observe that I am critical of the generalist concept basically because of its spurious theoretical basis and its narrow outlook.

The Interaction between Planners and Sociologists

From these concepts of the "generalist" and the "contributor" one could deduce some qualities of their interaction which one could then expect to see, if only to a certain degree, verified in the reality of the professional relationship between sociologists and planners:

(1) The planner will seek to *dominate this interaction*. The sociologist will be restricted to an *instrumental* role. The planner will maintain that a planning qualification is the only way of entry into a fully recognised position in planning.

(2) The planner will emphasise those aspects of his work which are the bread-and-butter of his position, namely the statutory planning process. Here, in particular, he will *resist the involvement of the sociologist* and any critical examination of

[4]Professor R. H. Kantorowich, Education for Planning, *Journal of the Town Planning Institute*, 53: 175-84, May, 1967.

the institutions and practices which flow from it.

(3) In an unreflective manner, the planner will be *aware of the poverty of his discipline*, an awareness which will lead either to defensiveness or to frustration or both.

(4) The sociologist will show more conscious awareness of the lack of planning theory and of the fact that his own discipline could potentially contribute something in this very field. He will therefore feel *frustrated about the restricted role* that is accorded to him.

In what follows I can do no more than give, within the constraints of time, a few illustrations of the ways in which these conclusions are borne out by the experiences of sociologists in their collaboration with planners. I do this with all caution and fully aware of the limitations of my material to which I have referred before. Verification will certainly have to wait for an investigation of quite a different kind which, it is hoped, could eventually build on this material.

Empirical Findings

The expectation that the planner tends to dominate the professional relationship with the sociologist is borne out in at least three ways. One is the instrumental role accorded to sociology itself to which reference has already been made. Another is the isolation and the low grading of sociologists in local authority planning departments, and the last the fact that, where sociologists want to rise beyond the most insignificant levels they are expected to take a graduate planning course.

A good many references were made to an instrumental view of sociology. Asked about the planners' view of the purpose of sociology some answers were: "... they want the sociologist simply to provide them with information and *not* to bother them with his opinions. . . ."

"They think it's a *research tool* . . . descriptive. It will tell them what the social field is, in which they are acting, but it won't actually inform their decisions."

This view of sociology as that of a "technological handmaid" is further illustrated by the prominence of the idea of the *social survey* which the respondents overwhelmingly found with their planning counterparts. Two characteristic reactions were: "The main thing is, of course, the *social survey*: The idea that, if you have defined a problem of any kind, you rush out with your little questionnaire, collect data, and come back with some answers. . . . The identification of sociology with the social survey is really embarrassing. . . ."

"They perceive people going round and asking questions which the . . . physically oriented planner would like to know. They won't conceive of a creative intervention by the sociologist. They regard the sociologist really as a sort of non-price *market researcher*, finding out things which they want to know."

This view, although arising out of a specific attitude of the planner, also reflects popular misconceptions. As one of the respondents who had been called in as a consultant on a multi-disciplinary planning study indicated, it was even held by a consultant economist who was reluctant to admit to the usefulness of having a sociologist on the team because it was "no use doing these surveys". It was, however, depressing to see that some sociologists who had observed the operations of local planning authorities more closely reported a level of understanding of the methods of sociological research which had *not even reached* the stage of social surveys. One respondent with a wide view of the field observed: "There is one view which is that sociology is simply a tool and you will find . . . some authorites where a person called a sociologist is a junior woman in a small room who gets out *census material*. . . ."

This was confirmed by some of those who had been through this experience themselves: "At the time when I was working in planning it was assumed that most of the research was *statistical* and would draw on secondary sources. . . ."

"They used us primarily for *digging out statistics* and routine analysis and they failed to make use of the primary tool of our trade which I would suggest is the social survey."

Given these attitudes, it is not surprising that many respondents felt their skill to be under-used. This was reflected in general comments of the following kind: "While I worked with planners they *failed totally to use my training in the social sciences*. . . . They used their social scientists at that time merely as general purpose research workers without using their special skills. . . ."

There were also more specific complaints about ways in which sociologists were asked to provide supportive evidence for pre-conceived ideas, demands which contravened the ethics of research. This is how one respondent described such an incident: "When I first arrived in the planning department I was rather shocked at one stage to get a note from the head of the planning section to do research to *show* that people prefer to live in low-rise buildings rather than tall flats. . . ."

Add to this striking example of an instrumental view of social research the fact that sociologists are seen as public relations experts with "ideas about how to make people accept schemes" allied to the requirement as laid down in the 1968 Act for local authorities to exercise public participation in planning, so that this will become of increasing importance, and you have the view of the sociologist as an opinion-pollster/statistician, who is subservient to the planners in having to provide the rationales for their ideas and to sell them to the "people" who, it seems, are *his* professional expertise.

Frustration was shown by my respondents, in the first instance because of the isolation and rejection of their approaches from their planning counter-parts. Comments such as the following were fairly typical: "I am able to gloss over the difference and to shrug my shoulders and almost let them. . . . I am a big defeatist, if they are not going to accept what I say, well then, let them get on with it. . . . The main problem is, if you are *one sociologist* and the rest of the team has a planning orientation, there are going to be problems of mere 'shouting power' almost."

"It is not terribly pleasant, as it appeared, for weeks and months to continue an argument with colleagues who *somehow don't see your point-of-view as you see theirs. . . .*"

Irritation does not only result from a rejection of one's approach, it has also more tangible reasons. The opportunities for sociologists in local planning authorities are extremely limited. There doesn't seem to be a place for a sociologist on a higher grade-level. This may well be a reflection of the fact that it is not immediately apparent how sociologists *could* be of great use in planning or, indeed, of any use at all. Be this as it may, this restriction effectively prevents the build-up of experiences in the field of sociology and planning. Those sociologists who are tucked away in some research section of a planning department — itself an institution which drew some fire — are often anxious to get out at the earliest opportunity. Note the following report from somebody who went from a planning department into a social development department, amongst other things because he "wanted to be in something which had a 'social' label": "It was all a question of TPI training. *Without a planning qualification it was tight,* both in terms of money ... and in terms of experience. ... I couldn't move up. Only junior level grades were reserved for specialists and there were very few chances of promotion. So, the specialists were isolated. This is discouraging for building up experience."

Another respondent echoed this feeling by saying that she would have left planning sooner or later if she had not left for personal reasons anyway: "I would have found it frustrating to continue as a middle-range adviser *called in at the end,* and I am sure that I wouldn't have stuck. ... ."

The TPI's own policy with respect to the entry of social scientists is that of letting them go through a conversion course. These courses are not postgraduate in character and, indeed, this is emphasised by proponents of this policy who want truly "post-qualification" courses in addition to these. They are rather of the kind of a potted undergraduate course with introductions into a number of fields. Where sociologists are appointed into planning offices, this is often done with the understanding that they would eventually go through such a conversion course and thus become planners. This met with a lot of objections from the respondents concerned. The following comments were received from people who had been through such conversion courses: "Once you become a planner, and this is my experience, you tend to *lose your social science background.* You don't have time to do the reading and to keep up in your specialised field. This is a great pity, because you don't get specialists in higher posts."

Two other respondents put it much more succinctly: "For what we want to do in planning, a planning diploma, as we did it, was *pretty irrelevant.*"

Another respondent who was in the process of doing a planning course said that he made this planning qualification "... basically because the planning profession is so organised that you *don't get very far in it without a planning qualification.* ... I don't think it ought to be necessary to do this. I don't think, quite honestly, that having done a planning course, one does one's work any better. ... You can go home in an evening or two and teach yourself some planning law if you are interested. I don't think that really justifies it. But as long as it is like it, most people who come in are going to get qualified. ... ."

It is more than just a vague feeling that had led this respondent into taking this course. This is what had happened in his planning department: "In this group that I am in there were four people eligible for promotion to group leader, two of whom are qualified AMTPI. All four people put in applications because it was reasonable that everybody should do so and everybody was encouraged to put in an application. But the choice was made from among the two who were qualified, and the other two, in fact, were *excluded* in the selection process. It's very real."

Passing on to the second of my propositions, the reluctance of planners to let the sociologist participate in decision-making, this attitude is evident where sociologists found that they had been called in too late, where, even though having been involved right from the beginning, they were not called in when a project took a decisive and unexpected turn, and in all other cases which showed that they were adjuncts rather than full members of a team. Conversely, where they somehow had managed to bring what *they* felt was their most useful faculty to bear, namely where they had criticised planning policy, they drew hostility. This puzzled some of my respondents who were used to the idea of academic argument and who valued this as a way of learning and advancing knowledge. Some relayed that, to their amazement, they had *not* found planners to be responsive to these challenges, nor had they, very often, been *asked* where misunderstandings had occurred on the other side.

Apart from the tangible interest which they have in maintaining their position what is underlying this reluctance of planners to allow sociologists to inform their decisions is the nature of their theory. This somehow assumes that decisions about policy and co-ordination arise from a close enough study of their subject-matter, the physical environment, for which they feel responsible. Only such an assumption enables planners to regard social inputs on *a par* with others. As one respondent commented, for planners there are "physical needs" and "social needs" which must both be fulfilled.

There is some evidence for the view that planners *are* aware of the poverty of this theoretical assumption which centres on the physical system instead of relating it to the *uses* to which this is put by human beings. This evidence is circumstantial because it is not based on first-hand data, nor were questions included in my survey which were aimed at establishing these facts about planners. In any case, some respondents did refer to at least two aspects of such an awareness which are defensiveness and frustration exhibited by planners.

Defensiveness is shown where, the lack of understanding about the nature, and by implication the applicability, of social theory notwithstanding, there seems to be apprehension about sociology as constituting a potential threat to planners. As one of the lecturers in my sample reported: "Their view of the social sciences seems to be rather hazy. . . . I don't think that there is a very clear understanding of what it's all about, apart from the fact that they seem to fear that there is a *certain threat* to their standing and position."

Another respondent perceived this with singular acumen: "In terms of their own discipline one had the feeling that *their backs were against the wall. . . .* Social scientists were threatening the old architect-planner, surveyor-planner and physical geography-planner. They were coming up with new methods of explanation of problems which these people did not understand. The notion was typically: 'We get so many inputs, there is no way of evaluating them all. What we must do is just to make the best choice possible. We do this because we are planners and because we have experience in making plans'. . . ."

But it was not only this sort of reaction which was shown. Some respondents found it significant that planners themselves were frustrated, disillusioned and even cynical about the political process, something which they found either incomprehensible or disdainful or both.

With the younger generation of planners — the generation-gap in the planning profession also drew much comment — there was an added source of frustration which was the *irritation with their superiors* which appears to be stronger than one might expect even in these days. Local planning authorities seem to be glorious hierarchies and not in vain does every statement about the planner as a "generalist" refer to him *in the singular*. In fact, younger planners are as much "contributors" as their specialist colleagues, only with substantially fewer employment opportunities outside and appreciably more chances of promotion inside the planning world.

Turning finally to the sociologists and their perceptions of planning, it was evident that they, almost invariably, found their collaboration with planners disappointing. They had many criticisms to make ranging from comments on simplistic and deterministic approaches to the fact that planners showed lack of understanding of people and had a middle-class and bureaucratic bias. In the final analysis their criticism mostly boiled down to one point which was the poverty of planning theory. Without this theoretical basis, they did not see much justification to the treatment they were subjected to, and not surprisingly the generalist concept drew much fire. The following is only one of the most characteristic responses. Jack-of-all-trades was mentioned much more often: "The pigeon-hole which they are framing for themselves is that of a *jack-of-all-trades*, a little bit of everything, with which they cannot compete with the specialist on any specific problem. They have got a *rag-bag sort of education* which has fitted them for next-to-nothing. . . ."

In conclusion, it is certainly fair to say that sociologists don't very often seem to *recognise planning as a discipline*. They don't do so in either of the following ways:

(a) They don't see planning as a distinctive field in its own right, but tend to regard anybody who acts in a planning sort of way as a planner.

(b) They do not see planners to have a discipline, to have theoretical rigour in the same way as they perceive their own profession to have a theoretical core.

This is really the basis for the claim frequently made by my respondents that sociologists, and by implication other contributors, ought to be at least *equal members of planning teams*. I say at least because some comments indicated that, in their hearts, a few of my respondents felt that, on the strength of his discipline, the sociologist would actually be a better team-co-ordinator than the traditional planner, certainly if planning were to be understood as something fairly broad and comprehensive, as having a high content of policy-matters, and not as the administration of development control alone.

Conclusions

The conclusions which I personally would be inclined to draw are, in the first instance, that this "generalist" concept of the planner's professional role is not only theoretically untenable but also harmful. Not that I would like to see the planning profession returning to its previous position where it was dominated by the "parent professions". Ridding itself of this mainly architectural predominance was a tremendous advance because it opened new avenues for a *social-science based profession of comprehensive planners* who would help increase the amount of scientific and technical intelligence brought to bear on the process of social guidance, not as philosopher-kings, but as change-agents, helpmates and catalysts with the highest sense of social responsibility. I very much hope that planning might take this course which would, at this juncture, require discontinuing restrictive practices such as those experienced by most of my respondents. Whether the professions could continue successfully maintaining water-tight compartments of professional competence in the hopefully more fluid situation of the post-Maud era remains doubtful anyway. The rationality of a narrow approach is therefore a questionable one, even in terms of professional self-interest.

The Position of Sociology Lecturers in Planning Schools

There are many pitfalls and frustrations of teaching sociology on planning courses. Some measure of tension certainly results from the nature of planning as an applied field and sociology as an academic discipline. But there is another dimension to this which is the position of sociology lecturers in the world of planning education and the way in which it influences their ability to make themselves felt, to have informal contacts with students, in particular during studio work, and generally to represent the viewpoints of the social sciences.

Questions concerning these matters were included in a mail questionnaire sent to lecturers in 1969. They will be analysed below under "Amount of Contact" with students which, by and large, appears to vary with the kind of employment (whether full-time, part-time or service-teaching), under "Experiences" and "Status of Sociology Lecturers", their "Involvement in Project Work" and, finally, in the "Supervision of Written Work". This will then bring us to the pros and cons of having full-time sociologists on the staff of planning schools.

Amount of Contact

Much seems to depend on the amount of contact which sociology lecturers have with their students. Some comments indicate that the lecturers in sociology are somewhat divorced from the mainstream of planning courses. The analysis of the twelve questionnaires returned by individual lecturers bears this impression out. Of these, six were in service-teaching, i.e. they were mainly employed by other than the planning department and gave their courses as a service under inter-departmental arrangements. Presumably these lecturers did not participate very actively in the determination of the objectives of their courses or of their place in the context of the curriculum overall. A further three are part-timers, two of them mainly teaching in separate institutions and coming into their planning schools from the outside. One lecturer is a housewife and mother with no other occupation besides her part-time teaching. Only three out of the twelve lecturers are full-time members of the staff of planning schools. Out of these, one holds a town planning qualification, another one has no formal qualification in sociology but holds a degree in architecture amongst others.

The difficulties of part-time and service-teaching have been emphasised by a number of respondents in personal interviews:

"There are difficulties of working in a service capacity to any other department. . . . It's a problem of organisation. . . . One, perhaps, is not really related in the way as it might be useful from the educational point-of-view. I think there could be much fuller integration and I am not altogether happy about the programmes in town planning at the moment. Sociology shouldn't be just a sort of service teaching. It should be more involved. . . . Too often, one doesn't hear of what they are planning until the very last minute. . . ."

"From the practical and administrative point-of-view it would be much better if I were part of the department. There are quite a lot of difficulties of a breakdown of communications. . . . I don't think . . . that bringing in a sociologist for a couple of days a week from a department which does nothing but service teaching is successful at all."

One of the lecturers concerned gave a description of how he had tried to operate as a service teacher and how this effort had failed:

"On one occasion I went . . . to have a chat with Professor X, and I wouldn't say he was particularly receptive to more collaboration. I suppose he has got to see the thing from an overall point-of-view. Sociology is just one of the many subjects which provide service teaching. We have no formal channel for influencing the structure of sociology teaching in their course, and our general view is that this should come from them. If Professor X was really keen then we would probably respond. But the way the department is organised we certainly don't feel we should be pushing ourselves too much."

The fact that service teaching is an unsatisfactory arrangement has been confirmed by two sociologists whom I interviewed in a different context. They had been through planning courses, and their comments are included as representing the consumer view:

> "We had a sociologist who came and lectured to us once a week for two years. But she had no planning background whatsoever. She was completely theoretical ... there was just no further contact. . . ."

> "One was given a very brief and schematic outline of all subjects, not only of sociology. . . . No real understanding at all."

The same respondent concluded that full-time sociologists should be appointed to the staff of planning schools:

> "Here, the onus lies largely with the education in planning. If it wishes ... to involve specialists ... planning schools should engage people who are fully qualified sociologists and who have had experience in sociology, possibly in planning, to be able to relate their experience and to teach their students accordingly. . . ."

This was seconded by lecturers:

> "A sociologist can only contribute to planning if he is actually in the planning process. In planning education, e.g., you can't have service teaching. You have got to be involved. . . ."

> "I think there should be full-time lecturers in sociology on the planning staff. I think this is the way it should be played, if only because of the chances of them obtaining from service teachers a degree of commitment to their particular problems being fairly remote."

Respondents who were actually on the staff of planning schools confirmed this. One of them described her work as virtually the same as that of other members of staff. It included the supervision of thesis work and studio projects. Another one described the way in which she was drawn into the decision-making process once she came into close contact with the development of the course:

> "A year ago I would have said, most definitely, that I was an outsider. But, in preparing CNAA documents, booklists and the syllabus, in being involved with the TPI recognition, I find that the head of school brings me in in most areas where matters germane to my areas of interest are discussed. . . ."

The negative effect of service teaching arrangements in terms of involvement in the decision-making process is reflected in a number of responses of those interviewed. One lecturer described it in the following way:

> "I am a specialist called in by them and I don't have the final say, so to speak. I am purely subsidiary, I am not complementary to the team."

The same person also reported that "they" had written her syllabus which had "all the right words" in it, but they had "jumbled them all up", and "it was not meaningful, sociologically speaking". Another respondent in the same position who, even though not having been given his syllabus, reported: "It's a very touchy point, indeed, but I don't take part in their staff meetings".

He, too, ascribed his disappointment to the lack of collaboration:

> "I certainly think there should be co-operation. . . . At the present level it's probably insufficient. Certainly, by giving them a course, I am helping, but I am under no illusion about the effects. . . . The examinations more or less mirrored what I have said in the lectures. . . . I say they didn't succeed very well with integrating sociology with planning. It's a pity. . . ."

In summary, the way in which sociology-lecturers are related to the structure of planning schools seems, in the opinion of most concerned, to influence their success, with the discontinuous nature of service and part-time arrangements on the debit side.

Experience

Another question in the mail-questionnaire concerned experiences in research and in planning education as well as numbers of years since graduation (first degree). Seven out of twelve have more than five years, two even more than ten years of experience since graduation. But not all this experience seems to have been relevant. Five of the lecturers indicated that they had less than one year's research experience in sociology, another three less than two years, and only one had more than five years of such experience. Nor does the majority have very substantial experience in planning education either. Only two of the sample had been through more than five years. Furthermore, research which the respondents had undertaken did not show any particular relevance to planning nor was there any consistency in the topics chosen. (Only race relations was mentioned twice.)

Some of the lecturers indicated that they were involved in teaching a number of other courses such as statistics, current affairs, social and political ideas, political economy, economics and public administration. This took up to 75% of their time.

The lack of experience which is strictly relevant to the teaching of sociology to planners was something which some of the lecturers interviewed were acutely aware of. One suggested:

"In education we have the difficulty still of making the link between sociology and planning. For this, it would be preferable to have a sociologist with a planning qualification and with planning experience on the staff to integrate the two...."

The same point was echoed by others:

"Basically, there is rather poor collaboration between the two, because sociologists, by and large ... don't really know what it is that they can contribute to planning...."

"I have absorbed a great deal of their concepts, and I am also understanding their impatience with other sociologists. What is actually required is very close collaboration over time...."

The Status of Sociology Lecturers

The general picture which emerges is that of service courses offered by outside departments which are passed on to more junior and sometimes less experienced members within these departments who then try to define their role and contribution within the framework of a pre-determined course. For quite legitimate reasons, these do not see their main career in planning education, which is however not to say that they are not interested or even enthusiastic about their role. But their orientation is towards sociology and they try to give as good an introduction into their field as they can. There is as yet certainly little indication of an opening for sociologists in the field of planning education itself so that they would be able to develop their contribution in more depth. As one of the part-timers commented: "Sociology should and could be an integral part of planning education, but planners will have to be convinced first."

A slightly more positive but still a mixed attitude on the part of planning staff proper comes through in the following comment:

> "I have got an intuitive feeling that planning staffs are anxious to see sociology on the course, but are, at the same time, rather sceptical as to its importance in the actual planning process. . . ."

This ambivalent attitude comes through where sociology lecturers, even though full-time on the staff, are restricted to a lecturer grade. As one respondent commented:

> "I have been very much aware of the lack of a senior representative of the social sciences. . . . Because of the power situation this has been refused at several occasions. . . . The view that social sciences were seen as contributory disciplines resulted in non-senior appointments of them. All social scientists are of lecturer grade although many of them have been here for some time. . . ."

If one compares the position of the lecturers in the hierarchy of teaching staff, one finds that a good majority of them, i.e. nine out of twelve, are on the level of lecturer. One additional one is an assistant lecturer at a university. Only one is a senior lecturer who is, however, only marginally involved in the teaching of sociology to planners in that he gives a course in social psychology within the framework of a social studies course and as a service-teacher. This marginal case apart, there is only one sociologist left who is in a senior position as principal lecturer and Deputy Head of Department, but he has full planning qualifications and many years of experience in planning, so that one may assume that it is this, rather than his qualification in sociology, which accounts for his senior position. Although grading in different educational institutions is not strictly comparable, the survey thus indicates clearly that lecturers in sociology are of junior grades with all the implications which flow from this for their ability to take a major part in planning their courses and for making an impact in their schools.

Involvement in Project Work

The involvement of sociologists in the organisation and supervision of project work adds to this picture. Project work takes the lion's share of planning students' time. It is cherished by planning educators as the core of planning courses. But only one of the twelve respondents to the mail-questionnaire has acted as year master or project supervisor. It is significant that he holds an architectural degree and therefore might be more readily accepted as a member of the planning staff proper. Another respondent with a full planning qualification indicated that he had been involved in the supervision of project work before becoming Deputy Head of Department. Only four of the respondents reported that they were in permanent co-operation with year masters or project-supervisors on certain specific projects, whereas nine answers were that occasional services had been sought from the respondents. Two of the twelve lecturers were not involved in project work.

The respondents were asked to comment on the type of their involvement. The greatest number indicated that they were engaged in designing questionnaires and supervising their administration. One lecturer described the "preparation, administration and analysis of two surveys (one village and one holiday) which have been used by students in planning village and holiday camp" as his role in project work. He also commented: "I think continuous co-operation between year staff and academic staff is crucial, particularly on project work" which allows one to infer that the co-operation did not actually take place. He also added:

"Students tend to use surveys as though they were market research. At this stage of their career that is not too bad, but the fact that they don't ever get back to sociology seems to preclude more sophisticated analysis in later years."

A senior sociologist/planner said that he supervised the construction of all questionnaires and their analysis. Another lecturer noted that his involvement was small: "Consultations usually take the form of requests for information of any sociologically relevant material." A further comment was that "general and very occasional advice on methods" was sought. Still a further comment read: "I have only been involved from time to time in assisting students to draft questionnaires for studies of towns and villages, existing conditions and planning proposals."

To sum up, involvement in project work is mostly a minor one and confined to the purely "instrumental" contribution of designing questionnaires. However a number of comments indicate that some of the lecturers want to be involved in a more substantial capacity than designing questionnaires, the use of which is beyond their control. One noted:

> "No involvement as yet but this is planned. Hope to be involved in all practical planning projects putting forward sociological considerations."

The same sort of attitude is reflected in the following statement:

> "As this is the first year the reconstructed Year II course has run and I am a part-timer, I have found it difficult to integrate myself into the frame. Next year it has been proposed that the sociologist helps set studio projects and directs them on *a par* with the others in an attempt to apply concepts usefully and not to teach in what (to planners) is an academic vacuum."

The importance which sociology lecturers attached to being involved in project work was also evident from interviews. Project work received most of the comments. These related to three areas. One was the need for integration. A second type of comment reflected a certain incredulity about the types of projects which those of the lecturers who were called in to assist in practical work found. Some respondents went even further in outlining the basic features of projects which they would run given the opportunity of organising their own projects.

The desire for being involved in project work was reflected in most comments. One lecturer replied when asked about involvement in project work:

> "Only in a peripheral sense: I have been in a number of meetings with planning students ... who were doing projects, and have discussed a number of issues with them. But nearly always it came far too late in the day to be useful at all. ..."

> "The only way of overcoming this mental barrier to integrating sociology in the students' own minds is by getting the sociologist more involved in their practical work. ... If the sociologist was invited to participate in their work, I think the experience of seeing how a sociologist would tackle a problem would be really valuable. ..."

Sometimes, the lack of integration between the teaching of sociology and project work goes as far as to prevent sociologists even from being called in on crits. Asked about the effect of his work on the way students thought about problems, one respondent answered: "If I was asked to come in on the assessment of studio work, it might be easier to assess one's impact." But some others who have been through this experience of being invited to criticise studio projects saw a need for a more intense form of involvement:

> "I have seen sociologists who found it a bit of a bore being invited to criticise projects, and who simply took a destructive line. Whereas, if you get somebody who is interested . . . to participate, leaning over their shoulders, it's better."

Some experiences suggested that such an involvement does have its pay-offs. A lecturer who reported that in his first year he "was not allowed to do any work with them", pressed to do practical work with students and subsequently had the feeling of success:

> "I made myself available to the students which I think helps, and I have been able to meet them outside the lecture-room."

It is only rarely, however, that a sociology lecturer is in the position of this respondent:

> "Last year I was in the lucky position of being in charge of a whole year. So I was able to design all their programmes. Obviously I gave a particular slant to it . . . if you are just called in, you have not got much influence."

In this case he did not feel that lack of a planning qualification constituted any difficulty:

> "I am involved in projects and I am asked questions with which I feel equally competent to cope as the planners."

But such a type of very close involvement can lead to strain, not so much with students but rather with other members of staff who may take quite a different approach. This is how the same respondent reflected on experiences in studio projects:

> "In crits I may tend to criticise things not as a sociologist, but because of my particular values, and this often leads to conflict. But this is the best way to show to students that planning is about values which people hold and not a dispute between disciplines like many people prefer to see it. . . . In a project on future towns, for instance, this really expanded into the role of the planner and also into political structure. They decided that the sort of city that they wished to create required a totalitarian system in which the planner

could impose his will, could shift population. This total control of environment made a present system of representation, indeed, any form of democracy, completely impossible if they really wanted to be able to create the sort of environment that they preferred. Obviously some people didn't think that this was what you should have people doing in studio work. They thought it was pretty irrelevant. . . ."

This difference in orientation which sociologists would adopt in studio work was reflected in the amazement which some showed about the naivity of architecturally orientated projects. Some of these comments were:

"Topics discussed came down in the end to simplistic architectural points about the presentation . . . of the students' work. . . . The projects were never designed to cover the broader social implications. . . ."

"Looking at their project work, one raises questions about, e.g., the type of houses provided and the reasons for it, which are couched in sociological ways of thinking. You get the answer: 'Oh, we never thought of it like that.' They think about these things in physical terms, tidy terms, if you like, without consideration of the deeper questions that they could ask. For instance, right in the middle of the scheme, a little block with three old people's flats. I said: 'Could you tell me why you have got the flats in the middle of this splendid housing scheme?' — There was no particular reason! — 'Why have you got two-bedroom houses and three-bedroom houses?' — Again no particular reason! — 'We were told that there should be a sort of mix.' — Purely in terms of numbers of rooms, sizes of dwellings or the appearance of things, not in terms of the population! . . ."

"Sociologists would be far more interested in looking at particular problems which a given plan posed . . . to the particular groups involved which . . . most of the planning students had only considered at the most superficial level, and the difference really was that, while they rushed around making noises . . . about the human factor and that planning is for people, when it comes to the pit, I don't think they have any clear idea at all as to how one actually builds this into their schemes. In the event, nine out of ten of the projects which I have seen paid only scant attention to the characteristics of the situation."

"You had these lads throwing up diagrams which took ages to do, showing the functions of housing . . . bedrooms, and what is done in bedrooms, etc., . . . and arrows showing movements outwards and inwards. . . . This seemed to me all to be a waste of time. . . . This emphasis on diagrammatic presentation and . . . neatness depressed me. Presentation for itself! . . . Some members of staff insist on it. . . ."

"The determinism of architects comes through where they control studio work, where major criticism tends to be in architectural terms" — e.g., one of the groups decided to provide a commuter village on the lines of New Ash Green for Leeds for the top 2% in terms of income, "and this was acceptable to the architects, because it's rather beautiful . . . and any idea of social responsibility was alien to them."

But, given the chance, what type of project would sociologists devise? One indication was given by a respondent who explained the way in which a misconception had arisen during his involvement in project work:

"Their idea was that in the third term we would be drawing together the different components of urban form and get the students to develop some theory of urban structure. . . . I discovered towards the end of the year that the engineer-planner and I had a completely different idea about what urban structure was. I took it for granted that urban structure was a set of relationships . . . between social factors. To him, urban structure was merely a communication-network."

Another respondent described the type of projects which he would prefer to run:

"I would like to see . . . sociologists to get involved in action projects. . . . They should select problems which have soicological aspects inextricably mixed up with structural problems, making an input here by showing that the demography of an area is a crucial determinant of the behaviour of those who live in it. . . ."

It would be interesting to explore this topic of the involvement of sociologists in project work further, but unfortunately the material on this is strictly limited, as we have seen the experiences of sociologists themselves are. One expects that most of the problems of the application of sociological theory would be reflected in this exercise and that the experience would be valuable — not the least to the sociologists themselves.

Supervision of Written Work

More use is made of sociologists in the supervision of written work than in projects. Five out of twelve indicated that they supervised written work of a more substantial nature (i.e. theses, etc.) but two of these in a somewhat minor role, i.e. for "clarification of concepts and data sources" in one case and as "co-supervisor" in the other. Three of the lecturers reported that they set topics and read students' essays. But written work seems to be somewhat alien to the whole concept of planning education through project work. This is a problem which sometimes makes sociology lecturers almost despair, such as the one who reported: "I try to get students to search out evidence. Again I am not always very successful. An awful lot of essays show very little evidence of reading . . .", and even: "You do get people, sometimes, who write material without any kind of grammatical structure. But usually I throw that sort of work out . . . and try to coax them into writing some sense. . . ."

This somewhat less academic orientation, as reflected in the poor quality of written work, is probably the result of the whole culture of some of the planning schools. A sociology lecturer who had been through a graduate planning course recalled:

> "The professor was demanding to see work on paper. He asked: 'Where are your plans? When will you get down to the drawing stage?' This was the war-cry. And the pressure was upon you to *produce*, no matter how much you thought about it."

With written communication, an area is touched upon where a secondary, but nevertheless important, objective of a course in sociology is conceivable. Sir Eric Ashby says about the social science element of engineering courses: "It is important that the course should be used as an opportunity for exercises in communication between students: for inarticulateness is an occupational disease among technologists. . . ."[1] With the recent emphasis on public participation in planning and the growing importance of, for example, the policy statement in planning under the 1968 Planning Act (where the structure plan consists mainly of this written statement and the plan document is only illustrative) the importance of communication is all too evident. Sociologists, on the whole, are more used to written communication than planners are and could thus fulfil an important function, marginal though it is to their own discipline.

Departments for the "Sociology of Planning"?

Much of what has been said about the position of lecturers in sociology indicates the desirability of having full-time sociologists on the staff of planning schools. In what follows, this will be balanced against the apprehension which some respondents showed about isolating sociologists from their academic peers. As some respondents to the interview survey remarked, individual sociologists tend to be lost in non-sociological departments. Although admitting to the importance of continuous interaction they were therefore against having individual full-timers on the staff of planning schools.

"Although, if you are arguing that you should have a permanent sociologist over there in the planning department, I would certainly disagree with you. There is an argument for having a service teacher who ... maintains his link with sociology, but who participates more than I do — one hour per week."

"I could do no fruitful work within the department in which I was employed. The teaching itself was very difficult because I was isolated as a sociologist amongst planners and this had all sorts of implications for the teaching of sociology." — (Asked about whether he could influence his terms of reference:) "They were so vague that they could be twisted in any way. But it was rather like twisting

[1]Eric Ashby, *Technology and the Academics — An Essay on Universities and the Scientific Revolution*, pp. 86-7, London 1963.

sponge-rubber. The department seemed to remain the same. Although I held two seminar-courses and I participated in a number of projects, this didn't affect the long-term development of the department."

This apprehension about being on one's own in an alien intellectual environment was evident even with those lecturers who had pleaded for the appointment of full-time sociologists:

"They might be bossed round. They need to be, to some extent, independent, and at the same time they want to be able to take part in creating programmes. . . ."

The difficulties which this creates notwithstanding, there is undoubtedly much to be said for full-time sociologists. This is not only because of the "instrumental" value of a sociological "input" into the "planning process", but because this could lead to change in planning itself. This is how one lecturer who was himself only marginally involved in the planning school, precisely because he was a service-teacher, saw the situation:

"It does seem to me that the chances for an advance in terms of an understanding of how planning affects people is going to come from the inside. It ought to come from the inside. It ought to be a question of planners mounting far more projects on the sociological aspects rather than on transport and aesthetics. . . ."

It is possible that those who have shown concern for the plight of individual sociologists in planning schools underestimated the contribution which a full-timer can make in a small department — and most planning departments are quite small in terms of size of the staff-establishment.[12] An albeit senior sociologist described his activities as full participation in the running of the department. He even filled the key-post of admissions-officer: "There are so few of us. We are all a sort of academic board. We all help to conceive an idea and plan it. . . ."

And he could describe as one of the results of his work: "A general atmosphere that takes into account the existence of sociology". This shows that there is some considerable scope for bringing a sociological viewpoint to bear, but it seems to be contingent upon experience and the

[12]The TPI's own requirement is six full-time members of staff. In 1968/9, the largest number reported by the planning schools was that of an establishment of 16 staff which, in 1970/1, has been superseded by at least one other school which is known to have a staff of 20 full-time lecturers.

standing of a senior member of staff in order to be able to endure a position of isolation. Where, however, departments grow bigger, another solution has been advanced:

> "I have a sort of vague feeling that, really, what one wants is bigger schools in planning. . . . It would be possible within these to build in not only the sort of traditional structure where you have people in different aspects of planning working side by side, but where you could also establish a number of, if you like, other departments within a planning school so that you wouldn't have a solo sociologist tucked away in a completely different environment. . . ."

Perhaps, with the increase of size of planning schools which is sometimes advocated, this proposal will become more feasible than it appears to be today. Some signs are encouraging. In most recent times, i.e. after this study was conducted, at least one senior appointment of a sociologist in a planning school has been made. The same school now has two full-time sociologists on its staff (together with other social scientists), which conceivably could form the nucleus of, if not a department, then at least a vigorous group overcoming the problems of lack of weight and of a position of isolation.[3]

[3]This problem of academic isolation appears to be nothing that is in any way restricted to sociologists and social scientists. Perloff and Friedmann, in their account of the Chicago experiment, describe how it was the physical planners who felt isolated in the environment of a social science faculty, and how this contributed in no small measure to the closure of the course in 1956. See Harvey S. Perloff (with John R. P. Friedmann): *Education and Research in Planning: A Review of the University of Chicago Experiment*, in: Harvey S. Perloff, *Education for Planning – City, State and Regional*, Baltimore, 1957.

Sociology in Planning Education [1]

This paper is about an issue ripe for consideration: the role of sociology in the planning curriculum. Everywhere, sociology forms part of planning education, but there has been relatively little discussion about how it should relate to courses overall. Those engaging in its teaching (Broady, 1969, 1974; Hübner, 1969; Reade, 1972) seem, furthermore, to lack a perspective on planning and planning education as areas of pursuit in their own right.

Sociology and the other social sciences, their potential notwithstanding, have failed to provide an adequate disciplinary base for those concerned with intervention in the real world. Such a disciplinary base is, however, being developed under different guises from policy sciences to design theory, with planning theory occupying a middle position somewhere between these two poles. Naturally, this new discipline perceives others as resources on which to draw. At the same time, the social-science disciplines (and sociology in particular) still regard intervention as in some respect their own legitimate territory. This results in an intellectual tension which is present in all forms of education for practical intervention (such as planning).

This paper draws on work done since the end of the sixties. At the outset, sociologists were interviewed about their collaboration with planners. The assumption was that their education should prepare planners for collaboration with other disciplines — what one might term an *inter*-disciplinary rationale. Since, at the time, planners had just resolved to treat other specialists as contributors rather than as partners, the reports on this work (Faludi, 1970, 1971) reflecting the frustration of those

[1]An earlier version of this paper has been published as Number 7 of the Working Papers in Planning Theory and Education, published by the Vereniging voor Studie-en Studentenbelangen te Delft at Delft University of Technology. One of its parts, i.e. the concept of an integrated educational knowledge code, was also the subject of a debate in the *Education for Planning Association Newsletter*, Vol. 4, Nos. 1 and 2.

concerned, were somewhat inimical to the planning profession whose development then became the subject of a subsequent paper (Faludi, 1972). But other work has led me since to supplement the inter-disciplinary rationale by another one, i.e. the view of planning theory as a (meta-)discipline in its own right (Faludi, 1973). This *meta-*disciplinary rationale provides the basis for later proposals concerning the curriculum.

Here, a disclaimer seems in order: the meta-disciplinary rationale for planning and planning education does not represent a return to the professional fold. Although dealing to a modest extent with professionalism and professional education, this paper is concerned with neither. The suggestion, at least for the undergraduate level, is to concentrate on relatively stable bodies of theory and on general skills and attitudes underlying any kind of practice in a complex and increasingly concerned society. The purposive selection of courses relevant to practical effectiveness in contemporary society is the most obvious line of advance, but perhaps not the most important one. The creation of learning and teaching situations for conveying the essential features of practice seems more important. These essential features are the pressure to synthesise disciplinary inputs into some programme of action, the need to cope with the inevitable pressure of time under which any such programme is formulated, and the reflectiveness of good practitioners concerning their own roles and achievements. In fact these amount to a *general capability to plan* which underlies so much of modern practice.

However, town planning education still provides a useful starting point for this discussion. After all, as an example of education for practice it has an outstanding tradition. If properly conceived, its central educational vehicle, project work, should prepare students particularly well for the general requirements of practice mentioned above. Its experience in devising situations for active and rapid learning under conditions of uncertainty even suggests that contemporary town planning education encapsulates features of a future type of general education for practical effectiveness.

The paper begins by presenting two concepts of how the various elements of a curriculum may hang together. Of these, the so-called integrated code seems preferable to the collection code. However, it raises the question of what is the core idea around which integration occurs. This question will be answered by proposing planning theory as a disciplinary core for planning education. Following from this, the role of sociology in a planning curriculum based on the view of planning as an emergent discipline in its own right will be explored.

The Collection versus Integrated Curriculum

Bernstein (1971) argues that the relationship between the contents of curricula units may be closed or open, characterising the collection and integrated curricula (or codes) respectively. The *collection curriculum* consists of a series of bounded and isolated subjects. Bernstein distinguishes between different variants from English specialised A-level subjects and honours degrees to the American non-specialised course-based type with its credit system. As against this, the *integrated curriculum* is one where previously isolated subjects or courses have been subordinated, to some relational idea, which blurs the boundaries between subjects. Again, there are different types, e.g., integration within and across subject-boundaries. Goodlad (1973), in a book dealing with the teaching of science to non-scientists (a problem which is to a certain extent analogous to the one of this paper), quotes the primary school "integrated day" where ". . . pupils are encouraged to exercise systematic curiosity . . ." as an example. Such an ideal, he says, ". . . is likely to emphasise *ways of knowing rather than states of knowledge*" with a tendency to undermine existing property rights in fields of knowledge.

It is indeed Bernstein's argument that the type of curriculum "affects the authority/power structure which controls the dissemination of educational knowledge": an educational institution based on the collection-code will be more bureaucratic and its teaching more didactic, and one based on the integrated code more egalitarian as regards the relationship both amongst staff and between staff and students. Moves towards integration will therefore be resisted because they implicitly threaten existing authority.

Now Bernstein certainly emphasises that "the specific application of the concept requires at every point empirical evidence". Nonetheless, this concept does suggest immediate applications in the interpretation of existing situations. Though carrying less weight than the application of a fully validated theory, such an interpretation may still help clarify the situation. This is presumably the spirit in which Goodlad uses the notion of various codes in explaining the "prestige problem" in science teaching for non-specialists at universities: the teaching of "general studies" to undergraduates in other disciplines is the poor relation amongst the activities of academic scientists with consequent effects on their willingness to teach non-specialists. The parallel with service-teaching of sociology to planners seems obvious.

In the process of separating from architectural education, planning education emulated a *collection code*. Outside critics[2] and bewildered students (Association of Student Planners, 1969) sometimes describe it unkindly as a "rag-bag sort of education" and its "product" as a "jack-of-all-trades". At its best, this type of planning education might represent one particular type of collection curriculum where different subjects focus on a common problem, in the case of town planning evidently the shaping of the physical environment. But the degree to which such focusing has been achieved in the teaching practice of planning schools is still an open question. Efforts to focus the teaching of the social sciences on the problems of physical planning were weak in Britain around the turn of the decade. As argued elsewhere, the so-called generalist concept of the role of the planner and the ensuing policy of the planning schools *vis-à-vis* their social-science staff were barriers to any such focused teaching (Faludi, 1970). They cast social scientists into the subordinate role of contributors, against which they reacted by defining their problem as that of attaining parity with their planning colleagues. In terms of the status of their disciplines they were seeking recognition for their autonomy rather than integration. To them, any step toward integration must have meant further domination by the established powers.

However understandable, this emphasis which sociologists in planning schools put on the distinctiveness of their discipline, is unfortunate because of the educational advantage of the *integrated code*. Planning students are being taught various disciplines, not merely because of the educational value of being exposed to them, but because of their alleged contribution to the student's effectiveness in practice. Responsibility for understanding how this occurs, however, is all too often shifted to

[2] See comments by social scientists in Faludi (1971) in this volume.

students who are expected to integrate subjects in their own mind. It is indeed scandalous that, instead of being told explicitly to what end and in what manner any one discipline can be used, students are being saddled with a problem which must leave them bewildered. This is the reason why the problem of integrating various disciplines seems of paramount importance in planning education.

Fortunately, the situation in present planning education is not quite as bleak as suggested. It clearly shows some features more reminiscent of integration. This is because what is taught in planning education gives it an in-built impetus for integrating subjects and teachers. To paraphrase Bernstein, implicitly an integrated "planning knowledge code" exists with effects on planning organisation and procedures analogous to those which he suggests flow from an integrated code in educational institutions: more horizontal relations amongst staff in the form of the many working parties which pervade current planning practice, and more exchanges between planners and the planned. Is it then surprising that those who venture to teach town planning also develop ideas about integrating the planning curriculum?

As an additional circumstance promoting integration in town planning education we may mention the existence of project work. In architecture and much of current town planning education, it is being seen as the most distinctly professional part of the educational programme, seeking to imitate, as far as possible, real-life professional experience. At the same time project work with its inherent flexibility provides educational innovators in the planning schools with a vehicle for trying out ideas, amongst others concerning the integration of disciplines. Many other institutions of higher education would find it difficult to match this opportunity. Project work is therefore a stimulus for, and a potential vehicle of, integration in town planning education, and the role of sociologists in project work thus a question of considerable importance.

The extent to which the coincidence of the integrated "planning knowledge code" with the availability of a suitable vehicle for integration (project work) has borne fruit is a matter for further research. The author has observed at least one school moving in this direction by adopting an approach to course planning analogous to the planning process (Bruton and Crispin, 1972, 1973), a procedure which, if taken to its logical conclusion, must lead to integration. One might conjecture that some degree of integration is also a feature of planning education elsewhere in Britain. Wherever integration occurs, it will raise questions about the "strong relational idea" such as Bernstein demands for any integrated curriculum, questions which the following section attempts to answer.

The Discipline of Planning

There are two reasons why the question of the discipline of planning tends to pose itself more sharply in *undergraduate* than in *graduate* planning education. Firstly, undergraduate curricula offer more of an opportunity to include courses on the various subjects deemed to be of some assistance to planning. However, in this way the unsatisfactory features of a collection code and the need for integration around a base discipline become more obvious. Secondly, undergraduate students have a greater need for a disciplinary base upon which to develop their intellectual identity than graduates who may simply regard planning as an area of application of their base disciplines.

Although some undergraduate planning courses exist elsewhere (for instance in the US, in Germany, Austria and, in some modified form, also in the Netherlands) Britain is the country in which they are by far the most prominent. This reflects the extent to which town planning has become professionalised in Britain. Indeed, the emergence of under-graduate planning education as the favoured, if not the only, form was part and parcel of the last phase in its professionalisation. Perceiving themselves to have been the target of a takeover bid from architects (as the most powerful of the professions operating in their vicinity), planners reacted by emphasising their distinctiveness. The feasibility of shaping an undergraduate programme was thought to increase the credibility of this claim (Kantorowich, 1967; Faludi, 1972).

This also shows how, by its very existence, a professional body like the Royal Town Planning Institute puts into focus the question of the disciplinary basis of planning, which elsewhere is allowed to remain dormant for somewhat longer. Discussions concerning such matters outside Britain, generally having fewer immediate implications for job opportunities and professional prestige, lack some of the punch which characterises the arguments concerning their discipline conducted by

British planners.

These two factors, the need to develop a disciplinary base for undergraduate planning education, and the speed and vigour with which developments in practice tend to be taken up in professional discussions concerning that same base, make Britain an exemplary case to discuss. Certain general features of the development of planning and their implications for both the profession and education are thereby well illustrated. The most important amongst these features is the diffusion of planning throughout public authorities and its role in efforts to achieve a greater degree of public sector coordination. Planning ceases to be the exclusive concern of individual departments (the situation which prompted Stewart (1969) to complain about too much rather than too little planning) and now attends more to linkages between the areas of concern of existing departments.

A concomitant change is the orientation of planning toward some form of overall guidance of all the activities of government. By becoming just one out of a number of professions which are prominently concerned with public planning, its distinctive identity is being threatened. At the same time, the greatest challenges in planning now tend to arise outside departments of town planning, i.e., where overall policy is being made. Not surprisingly, the top-flyers of the profession are particularly attracted by these new opportunities and are thus in the forefront of those wishing to broaden the commitment of the profession from just *town* planning to *planning* as such.

The pressures and counter-pressures described in the third essay of this volume on the changing scene of British planning education resulted in a new round of soul-searching within the Royal Town Planning Institute which ended with the emergence of a new educational policy in 1974. As has also been mentioned, the underlying logic of the new proposals is that of Perloff's "generalist-with-a-specialism" (Perloff, 1957). Because of its significance, the relevant passage of the discussion document *Town Planners and their Future* is worth repeating (The Royal Town Planning Institute, 1971): town planners should have "... a common core of professional expertise underlying one of a series of specialisations", this core consisting of: (a) planning methodology, (b) knowledge and understanding of the physical environment within which planning takes place, and (c) knowledge and understanding of the relevant administrative context and organisation. For the rest, there is freedom for innovation on "scale" (regional, local, etc.) or "subject" specialisms (transport, economics, design, etc.). Yet another Discussion Paper (The Royal Town Planning Institute, 1973) translated this into a "modular" approach to curriculum design combining "foundation" and "applied" courses, which became official policy (The Royal Town Planning Institute, 1974).

If we extend Perloff's "generalist-with-a-specialism" logic, then even this new core curriculum becomes one of a number of planning specialisms. There is, instead, a more central core which all of these have in common and which provides the basis for a broader "generalist" concept of planning divorced from any particular subject matter. Planning methodology may certainly be applied to handling problems other than those arising in the physical environment, and the administrative context embraces many more areas of concern than just this one. Knowledge and understanding of the subject matter concerned then becomes the variable element of a number of courses preparing prospective planners to operate in a variety of fields. This is but a small step from the current posture taken by the British planning profession.

For the larger educational institutions there are particular advantages in anticipating it. Such a step would promote cross-fertilization between teachers and practitioners in various fields. It would also help to remedy the existing imbalance in favour of physical planning education. The resultant broad-based "generalist-with-a-specialism" conception is, finally, intellectually most satisfying. It gives an unambiguous answer to the question of what the discipline of planning is, i.e. that body of theory which is underlying attempts at planning in a complex world of overlapping institutional areas of concern and conflicting interests, irrespective of subject matter. In somewhat uninspiring but nevertheless accurate terms, the documents quoted above term it planning methodology and the administrative context. My own preference goes for planning theory which, elsewhere, I describe as concerned with planning agencies and procedures (Faludi, 1973). Henceforth, the core discipline of planning will therefore be referred to as planning theory. It is an inalienable element of any planning curriculum. In the case of a basic curriculum on planning *per se* (followed by specialisations at advanced level in particular areas of its application) it is co-extensive with the core. Since the issues of integrating sociology into the planning curriculum are best elucidated using this type of curriculum as an example, the remainder of this essay will limit itself to discussing such a course. With little modification, the lessons are then applicable to other planning courses as well. However, before developing this train of thought, a few observations seem in order about sociology and planning conceived as a general activity.

Sociology and Planning

The use of insights gained from theoretical disciplines for the formulation of action programmes is a central problem for planning. Planners must therefore make it their concern to study issues raised in the application of knowledge. This emphasises the sociological and, more generally speaking, social scientific aspects of planning theory. The issue of relating knowledge to practical concerns permeates the development of sociology[3] and, if only to a lesser extent, the other social sciences as well. The famous argument on value freedom by Max Weber was indeed couched in terms of the social sciences and not just sociology.

The basic issue is indeed the same in planning as in the social-sciences: whether, and if so how, to differentiate between arguments backed by evidence and those appealing to what we think ought to be. In the planning literature, this debate is often couched in terms of ends and means. There are analogies here between the position of social scientists and of planners or administrators. For all of them the problem is to define proper conduct in a situation where they have much *de facto* authority in pronouncing on matters of policy.

Beyond this question of value judgements, scores of methodological issues become important for planning. Planning is becoming a prolific generator of social research. The question of how to distinguish reliable findings from unreliable ones ought therefore to concern planners. This refers to the formulation and testing of hypotheses, to problems of measurement, concepts of time and space, and so forth. Forecasting is another area where the common methodological problems of the social sciences are becoming particularly evident (Young, 1968) and which is

[3]As Simey (1961) says: "It is often forgotten today that it is the concept of purpose and of the enhancement of welfare that provided sociology with its starting point. . . .".

highly relevant to planning.

As against these social-scientific ones, the particular contributions of sociology to planning are of two kinds: those relevant to the planner's self-understanding, and those helping him to understand the phenomena he is dealing with. The sociology of knowledge and organisation theory make up the first: the former because the social determinants of knowledge ought to concern a discipline devoted to studying its application, the latter because planning occurs in organisations and comes to fruition through organised efforts. These two fields, which jointly form what has sometimes been referred to as the sociology of planning, help the planning theorist to identify obstacles in the way of formulating valid knowledge, or of validly applying such knowledge as is available. They also assist in providing favourable conditions for the articulation of planning programmes in creative team efforts.[4]

It is plain that these issues for which planning theory must draw on sociology and the social sciences cannot be avoided by the planner seriously concerned with enhancing the validity of planning decisions. Any perusal of the planning literature will indeed show planners arguing hotly about ends and means, about their relation with politicians and the public, about ideological distortions in the formulation of planning policies, and about desirable forms of planning organisation.

But the planner must not only remove the "thought blockages" (Beer, 1966) in the institutions of planning, he must also harness *all* available, relevant knowledge for understanding his *subject matter*. For the pursuit of practical ends in whichever field of public policy, the knowledge base must therefore always incorporate some sociological perspective. This is because planning links substantive knowledge to the purposes of an often diverse clientele. It cannot but incorporate an image of society.[5] For an intellectually satisfying image a sociological perspective of man as enmeshed in, and partially constrained by, a complicated network of relations with his fellow men is indispensable, just as Fletcher (1971) says: ". . . sociological theory is a subject of the greatest fascination — relevant

[4]Examples are given by Broady (1968); on "creative planning" and its conditions, see also Faludi (1973).

[5]For several demonstrations of the need for a sociological perspective in one of the most recent areas of great political concern, air pollution, see Downing (1972).

to almost any question that can be raised about man and his concerns. . . . It is a subject which stems from, and attempts to satisfy, the modern need to articulate all human knowledge into one large, ordered perspective both for the sake of *understanding*, in itself, and to provide a basis for sane and well balanced social *reform*. It is the subject of central importance in and for our time." The contention is therefore that planning programmes in fields like (to return to physical planning) housing, industrial location or transport should view the issues underlying as related to social and institutional structure. The same goes for all other fields of public policy.

Sociology in the Planning Curriculum

How are we to conceive of these ideas being put into educational practice? How are we, in particular, to cope with the problem that although sociology seems such an important element of any planning curriculum (contributing, amongst others, directly to the development of planning theory), its representatives are sometimes unwilling to contribute towards the effectiveness of planning? The proposal here advanced is designed to solve this problem over time.

There is an underlying message concerning conflict in the curriculum which should have wider applicability than just the area of sociology in planning education. This is that often conflict cannot be resolved in a mutually satisfactory manner. Since teaching goes on, rather than waiting for pressing issues to be resolved, one should therefore create structures within which intellectual conflict may articulate itself, and where the resolution of conflict may feed into the continuous development of a course. Underlying this message is yet another view of what a curriculum is, and what integration within a curriculum means. A curriculum in terms of a syllabus and regulations governing admissions, advancement and the award of qualifications is but the surface of something very much more complex, i.e. a delicate web of social relations amongst those concerned with a particular course. The intellectual relations between the individual elements of a curriculum clearly form but one out of a number of factors influencing curriculum development in general and integration within a curriculum in particular. To approach curriculum development and the integration between disciplines as a purely intellectual task is therefore a recipe for failure. Integration means, in particular, integration of people and their socialisation into some loose system of values. It is a delicate process always carrying the risk of failure, and in any case one that requires time, constant attention and care to trigger off and maintain.

As a vehicle for presenting the following ideas, a scheme for a general planning course dubbed Planning Studies is used. It has three levels. Each one of these might cover one or more years. For the present argument, length of study is unimportant. Each of the levels would have its distinct character. The first would emphasise formal teaching and have only limited, and carefully controlled, project work. The second and third would feature open-ended learning in small groups working on projects and special options. There is also an individual research paper during the final part of the course. More details are given in Appendix 1.

As regards the teaching of sociology and the social sciences, the principle underlying the scheme is to allow the tension between them and planning, viewed as disciplines in their own right, to work itself out. In recognition of their nature as separate disciplines, the *first-level social-science courses* should therefore be devoted entirely to expositions of their main paradigms, their methods of enquiry and main findings with no requirement to emphasise their relevance to planning.

This is not a token recognition. The independent position for the social sciences acknowledges the possibility of an impetus for better planning coming from any one of them. Besides, courses in the social sciences would also serve general educational purposes, just as introductory social science courses in various degree schemes replacing the classics as the avenues to liberal education do (Donnison and Chapman, 1965). Also, every planning student would be introduced to the language of each of the social sciences.

Whilst pursuing its main objective of studying planning, the *planning theory* course in year one should on the other hand indicate those issues where any one of the social sciences might *help* planners. For instance, the evaluation of alternatives is where economics comes in; the identification of organisational constraints on decision-making is a province of sociology; the relations between people, politicians and planners one mainly of politics. Only, this time, their presentation would be slightly less open-ended: to show how, and to what extent, we may evaluate alternatives; to reduce organisational "thought blockages"; to create smoother exchanges between the various participants in planning. Whilst the spirit would still be that of genuine enquiry, its purpose would now flow from the purpose of planning itself and *not* derive from within the discipline.

On the second level, the relation would be a similar one. *Planning theory* would continue pursuing its objectives of studying planning. Besides, each student would select one *social-science option*. But, whereas the previous social-science courses emphasised their diversity, each outlining its particular way of explaining phenomena, the options should stress what the social sciences have *in common*. As argued above, the application of each of the social sciences tends to raise the same issues of methodology and scientific ethics which, furthermore, are central to planning as the harnessing of knowledge for practical ends. Each of these options would therefore contribute in its own way to allow this scheme to go *beyond* the idea of the social sciences as "contributory disciplines". Rather than merely contributing, each one of them has an essential part in the development of the intellectual base of planning.

The development of such options should be a great opportunity for the tutors concerned. But options will take time to mature. Tutors not only require a thorough grounding in their own discipline, but also an unusual degree of familiarity with questions of methodology, and, last but not least, some sympathy for planning. These are difficult requirements to combine.

Next to core-curriculum and options, *projects* would be a prominent feature of the proposed course. These distinguish planning education. Their strength is that they involve elements of group work and that they foster decisiveness and the willingness to cope with practical constraints and with risks.[6] With appropriate care, projects can at the same time be academically demanding *and* simulate some essential features of practice.[7] It is therefore very important that sociologists (and other social scientists as well) should *participate fully* in project work and thereby avail themselves of the opportunities which it offers for demonstrating the relevance of their discipline in situations which come

[6]The advantages of "learning by doing" are being discovered in the field of management education. See Solem (1972).

[7]See Faludi, 1973, chapter 14. See also Part II of this volume.

close to the everyday world of planning.

Finally, the *joint planning methodology seminar* on the most advanced level needs to be described. This is designed to fuse the social sciences with the core teaching in planning. It would explore issues of common interest on the frontiers of planning and the social sciences, amongst others developing the work done in the social science options. The methodology seminars would also provide an avenue for discussions amongst staff which are vital for the development of any academic institution, let alone one bent on integrating various disciplines. In due course, as issues are resolved and new ones discovered, these discussions should become a main impetus for the continuous development of the whole course.

Overall, the balance between instrumental contributions of the social scientists on the one hand, and the independent role which they have in this scheme on the other, reflects the complexity of the relations between the social sciences and planning. It also complements the view which writers in this field tend to agree upon: that there exists a multitude of roles for social scientists in planning. Once this scheme had come into operation, we should add the planner himself who would then have a disciplinary base in planning theory and who would use social-science methodology, as well as substantive research findings, in pursuing the aim of better planning.

The arguments advanced previously in terms of the social sciences generally apply to sociology more than to any of the others. Sociology has always concerned itself most prominently with the general issues of methodology which this study emphasises. A sociologist might therefore be expected to respond more readily and more successfully to the challenges posed by this scheme than a graduate of any other of the social sciences.

Sociology would be offered, firstly, in form of a *basic course on sociological explanation*. Secondly, there would be an optional *sociology and planning* course on second level which, much as the other options, should focus on rationality, value freedom and research methodology, but also on more specifically sociological contributions to planning (e.g., organisation theory).

Sociologists would further contribute from time to time to planning theory and techniques courses and the final year seminar on methodology (for details see Appendix 2). Most important, however, would be their involvement in project work. There are three ways in which they could participate. Since this scheme tends to blur the distinction between planning teachers and social-science staff, sociologists could firstly act as *project coordinators* i.e. in a capacity of major responsibility for the development and implementation of particular projects. There is no need to limit such a role to projects with a particularly sociological bias. As argued above, in principle there are sociological aspects to all types of real-life problems. If no such aspect can be discovered, the project is, more likely than not, about a problem with low reality content.

In any case, the role of project-coordinator casts the sociologist in the mould of a planning teacher which, for the sake of further understanding and integration, seems highly desirable. The more frequent role for the sociologist would however be that of *contributor to project-initiated lectures and seminars*. The latter would be one of the ways for project groups to acquire the knowledge base required for solving the problem under consideration in a project. As a further variant of this theme, sociologists would finally become *in-house consultants* for project groups embarking on small research projects of their own. Detailed descriptions of these three roles are given in Appendix 3.

Conclusions: The Price of Integration

Such are the proposals of this paper which, it is hoped, will do justice to sociology and the other social sciences as disciplines in their own right whilst at the same time assisting students to form concepts and attitudes conducive towards intervention in a practical context. They are based on a preference for an *integrated* over a *collection* curriculum, on a view of *planning theory* as the *core discipline* for an integrated planning curriculum, on an argument that *sociology* (as indeed the other social sciences) makes *essential* contributions both to planning theory and to our understanding of the problems at hand, and on certain general ideas concerning planning education as a fascinating field for educational experiments. A conscious attempt has been made to promote integration by (a) offering vehicles for it in the curriculum, and (b) putting social-science staff on *a par* with their planning colleagues so that there should be no authority structures restraining free exchange of ideas.

Of sociologists, their involvement as sketched out above requires great versatility and command of their field. It also requires maturity in at least two respects: firstly, they need to accept the limitations which any one role imposes. Sociologists perceive criticism as a useful vehicle for advancing understanding. The scheme which I propose provides ample opportunity for exercising it in the proper context of theoretical pursuit. At other times it requires acceptance of assumptions derived from other concerns. In this way, the scheme strikes a balance between criticism and commitment to action. Elsewhere I have argued that the establishment and maintenance of such a balance is one of the problems in planning (Faludi, 1973). It is therefore not surprising that this notion should permeate this scheme for a planning course and that it should also apply to sociologists.

Secondly, participation in this scheme requires maturity in yet another respect. Some of the many positions in sociology are more conducive towards the ends of planning than others. The sociologist in planning education should certainly be free to deal with all of them, but he should also point out those which are complementary to the position of the planner. For instance, the sociologist who argues that there can be no planning under a capitalist system[8] raises a theoretical problem of great fascination which needs further inquiry. But, in the meantime, planners continue to assume that their approaches do make a difference for the achievement of practical ends, capitalist system or not. By and large, planning students also come into planning thinking that something can be done here and now. The general assumption upon which the sociologist enters into planning education is that he will assist them to find out how.

As Bernstein argues, any integrated educational code requires a level of consensus about the integrating idea. This is the price to be paid for the educational advantages of integrated learning and teaching. The sociologist with his reflective capacity should have the maturity to figure out for himself whether he can square the ameliorative ethos which permeates planning with his intellectual position. If, in all honesty, his sole purpose in teaching planners would be to make students aware that at present there is no such thing as planning, then he might find himself in an ethical quandary. Should he insist on thrashing this issue out, even at the cost of

---

[8]The German planning literature abounds with statements to this effect. See for instance Fehl *et al.* (1972).

incapacitating students for the type of practice they had chosen for themselves? No one can take this decision for him. One can only hope that it will be taken with due concern for the students he teaches.

To what extent planning schools should enter into these considerations in determining their staffing policy remains an open question. Reactions to one of the forerunners of this paper have cautioned me in suggesting that they should for instance take account of applicants' intellectual positions. The dilemma between adhering to the standards of academic freedom allowing knowledge to develop wherever it may take you, and the insistence that students should obtain an education which is relevant to their chosen area of concern (misconceived though their choice might be in the eyes of academic critics of current practice) is even greater for the schools than for potential lecturers. But practice, including the practice of educational policy in which one is engaged as a member of a selection board, does involve dilemmas of this kind. Having exposed it is perhaps the most a paper like this can do.

Appendix 1

THE MODEL SCHEME

As stated in the main text, the model scheme for an undergraduate curriculum in planning consists of courses on three levels. On the first level, it features a range of introductory lecture/seminar courses in *planning theory* and *techniques*, as well as courses in the *social sciences*, in *mathematics, statistics* and *computing*, and a sequence of *projects*. The second part retains only *planning theory* and *techniques* as compulsory lecture/seminar courses. Apart from these, students divide their time between one *option* in the *application of one social science to planning* and one *project*. On the third and final level they attend *joint staff-student seminars in planning methodology*, and for the rest of their time do an *individual research paper* relating to their social science option, and a *further project* in a group with others.

The whole curriculum is about planning as a way of preparing and implementing public policy programmes. The core courses in *planning theory* and, arising out of it, *planning techniques*, on first and second level, make it their central concern to study and develop planning in all its ramifications. But the social sciences have an equally important role to play. The *basic social science courses* should therefore be devoted to an exposition of their nature as disciplines, and the *social-science options* to the study of their application to planning. The *individual research paper* on third level is an extension of the work done in the chosen social science option. It completes the social-science curriculum extending over all three levels, thus giving adequate scope for studying one of them in depth. At the same time, the requirement that options should emphasise the features common to all the social sciences should give students the ability to cross the boundaries between them. The *seminar in planning methodology*, in which social science tutors should participate alongside with their planning colleagues, is finally designed to blur the distinction between planning subjects and the social sciences.

Great store is being laid in this model scheme on *project work* accompanying formal teaching. On the introductory level, projects include a carefully planned sequence of small problem-solving exercises attending, amongst others, to questions of group work, communication, etc. Their purpose is to prepare students for future projects and, incidentally, also to promote cohesion amongst them.

On the second level, project work begins in earnest. The topics set are fairly conventional planning problems as they occur in a public authority, i.e. the preparation and submission of a statutory plan document such as a structure or local plan, a school building programme, a social development plan, etc. However, because of the absence of courses on any substantive area of concern, these projects will require students to engage in self-directed learning. There might be short courses to introduce them to their problem areas. But all further activities will arise out of the project itself, with "student-initiated" lectures and seminars, site visits and discussions as the vehicles for acquiring insights into the substantive problem at hand. This would emphasise the central point of project work of studying and practising planning which includes, amongst others, the ability to learn rapidly. The selected topic of study, and the acquisition of knowledge thereof, are but vehicles for achieving this end.

The final project is different from the previous one only insofar as the range of problems investigated is concerned. As against the former, this one should investigate issues cutting *across* institutional boundaries, with all the difficulties which this entails for planners having to serve several masters at once (see Institute for Operational Research, 1971; Friend *et al.*, 1974). But the educational approaches used would be no different from those in the previous part.

Appendix 2

SOCIOLOGY CONTENT OF THE MODEL SCHEME

Basic Course in Sociological Explanation (First Level)

The introductory sociology course emphasises the nature of sociology as invoking social structure to explain a certain range of phenomena, including those of social change, thereby substituting "causal analysis for demonology" as Rex and Moors (1967) put it so aptly. It also seeks to equip students with what Sprott (1968) thought was one of the main results of studying sociology: the "habit of thinking about any social phenomenon in the social context in which it is found". Whilst clearly important for the professional, this aim has wider, educational importance, i.e. "to make human beings more aware of their social situations, more critically self-conscious and thus more fully human" (McRae, quoted after McGregor, 1961).

Sociology and Planning Option (Second Level)

The optional sociology and planning course focuses on the ideal of rationality in sociological thought; on the issue of value freedom; on social determinants of thought; and on organisation theory, as well as on general questions of research methodology.

Research Paper (Third Level)

The research paper for those who have previously taken the sociology and planning option involves them in a modest research project on a topic within this general area.

Sociologists should further contribute from time to time to planning theory and techniques courses and the final year seminar on methodology:

Planning Theory (First and Second Level plus Methodology Seminar, Third Level)

In planning theory, they might cover aspects relating to the same issues as mentioned above, i.e. rationality, value freedom, the sociology of knowledge, organisation theory, but basing themselves on case studies and other material drawn from planning practice. However, this time there are also other social scientists giving their interpretations of, say, the issue of value freedom. Furthermore, issues are now raised in the different context of a course entirely devoted to the study and promotion of planning. This provides the opportunity, and poses the challenge, for sociologists to make their case concerning the relevance of their discipline to planning.

Planning Techniques (First and Second Level plus Methodology Seminar, Third Level)

In planning techniques, sociologists deal with issues of research methodology and technique from basic problems of measurement to the practical ones of questionnaire design and analysis taking them further in the methodology seminar which would be open-ended enough to allow for most of the fundamental issues in the philosophy of the social sciences to be raised.

Appendix 3

ROLES OF SOCIOLOGY TUTORS IN PROJECTS

As Project Coordinators

As projector coordinators, their main perspective would be that of a planning teacher as such, i.e. to convey knowledge and understanding of planning and its approaches and techniques, and to instil attitudes conducive towards decision-making under uncertainty. Although this may not be to the liking of all sociologists, there is nothing to prevent some of them from taking on such a role, in particular (although not exclusively) where projects cover problems which sociologists have traditionally concerned themselves with, i.e. the social services, inner city problems, housing, etc. More frequently, sociologists would join small teams coordinating projects. In this capacity they should take the opportunity for developing sociological perspectives during the initial conceptual and final reflection phases of projects. They might also concern themselves with methodology and emphasise the importance of rigour in verbal communication.

Contributors in Project-Initiated Lectures/Seminars

Introductory courses into the sociology of substantive areas of concern, for instance housing, the inner city, welfare, etc., should be given on the initiative of the participants of a project and form part of their search for relevant knowledge about their area of concern. These should reinforce the point about developing a sociological perspective for understanding most phenomena with which planning is concerned.

In-House Consultants

This is the strictly consultative capacity of providing access to such knowledge and such technique as might be required for the achievement of specific ends in a project. The introduction of class variables into estimates of housing demand and housing satisfaction (Broady, 1968) or the explanation of commuting behaviour (Klages, 1966) are but two examples of such contributions of a relatively technical kind which the sociologist can make towards physical planning as one field out of many. Where relevant, this role also includes that of advising on small pieces of research undertaken in projects.

References

ASSOCIATION OF STUDENT PLANNERS (1969) *Aspects of Planning Education*, London.

BEER, S. (1966) *Decision and Control*. New York: John Wiley.

BERNSTEIN, B. (1971) On the classification and framing of educational knowledge. *Knowledge and Control* (edited by Young, M. F. D.). London: Collier Macmillan, pp. 47-69.

BROADY, M. (1968) *Planning for People*. London: The Bedford Square Press.

BROADY, M. (1969) Sociology in the education of planners. *SCUPAD Bulletin* (Salzburg Congress on Urban Planning and Development), No. 6, Sheffield, pp. 40-42.

BROADY, M. (1974) Sociology in the education of architects. *Architectural Association Quarterly*, Vol. 5: 49-52.

BRUTON, M. J. and CRISPIN, G. (1972) Project work – friend or foe? An approach to the design and development of project work for a first degree course in town planning. *Oxford Working Papers in Planning Education and Research*, No. 13, Oxford Polytechnic, Oxford.

BRUTON, M. J. and CRISPIN, G. (1973) Project work – friend or foe? *Journal of the Royal Town Planning Institute*, Vol. 59: 263-265.

DONNISON, D. V. and CHAPMAN, V. (1965) *Social Policy and Administration*. London: Allen & Unwin.

DOWNING, P. B. (1972) *Air Pollution and the Social Sciences*. New York: Praeger.

FALUDI, A. (1970) Sociology in planning education. *Oxford Working Papers in Planning Education and Research*, No. 4, Oxford Polytechnic, Oxford. (For an excerpt see the previous essay in this volume.)

FALUDI, A. (1971) The experiences of sociologists in their collaboration with planners. *Uses of Social Sciences in Urban Planning*, Seminar Proceedings, Planning & Transport Research & Computation Co. Ltd., London. (Included in this volume.)

FALUDI, A. (1972) The "specialist" versus "generalist" conflict. *Oxford Working Papers in Planning Education and Research*, No. 12, Oxford Polytechnic, Oxford. (For an excerpt see the second essay in this volume.)

FALUDI, A. (1973) *Planning Theory*. Oxford: Pergamon.

FEHL, G. *et al.* (editors) (1972) *Planung und Information*. Bertelsmann Fachverlag, Gütersloh.

FLETCHER, R. (1971) *The Making of Sociology*, Vol. 1. London: Nelson.

FRIEND, J. K. *et al.* (1974) *Public Planning: the Intercorporate Dimension*. London: Tavistock.

GOODLAD, J. S. R. (1973) *Science for Non-scientists*. London: Oxford University Press.

HÜBNER, H. (1969) Sociology in the education of town planners. *SCUPAD-Bulletin* (Salzburg Congress on Urban Planning and Development), No. 6, Sheffield, pp. 43-48.

INSTITUTE FOR OPERATIONAL RESEARCH (1971) *Beyond Local Government Reform*. Conference Proceedings. London: Tavistock Institute.

KANTOROWICH, R. H. (1967) Education for planning. *Journal of the Town Planning Institute*, Vol. 53: 175-184.

KLAGES, H. (1966) Arbeitsweg und Berufsverkehr – Soziologische Aspekte der

Stadt- und Verkehrsplanung. *Planung, Bau und Betrieb des Schnellverkehrs in Ballungsräumen.* Berlin: Bauverlag.

McGREGOR, O. R. (1961) Sociology and Welfare. *The Teaching of Sociology to Students of Education and Social Work* (edited by Halmos, P.). Sociological Review Monograph, No. 4, Keele, Staffordshire, pp. 33-44.

PERLOFF, H. S. (1957) *Education for Planning – City, State and Regional.* Baltimore: Johns Hopkins.

PROGRESS IN PLANNING (1973) *Education for Planning.* Report of a Working Group at the Centre for Environmental Studies, Vol. 1. Oxford: Pergamon, pp. 1-108.

READE, E. (1972) Sociology in planning education. *Official Architecture and Planning,* Vol. 35: 783-784.

REX, J. and MOORE, R. (1967) *Race, Community and Conflict.* London: Oxford University Press.

SIMEY, T. S. (1953) The contribution of the sociologist to town planning. *Journal of the Town Planning Institute,* Vol. 39: 126-130.

SOLEM, A. R. (1972) Role playing in management education. *Management of the Urban Crisis* (edited by Seashore, S. E. and McNeill, R. J.). London: Collier Macmillan, pp. 443-461.

SPROTT, W. J. H. (1968) Foreword, *The Strategy of Social Enquiry* (Wakeford, J.). London: Macmillan, pp. 6-8.

STEWART, J. D. (1969) The administrative structure of planning: 1. *Journal of the Town Planning Institute,* Vol. 55: 288-290.

THE ROYAL TOWN PLANNING INSTITUTE (1971). *Town Planners and their Future: A Discussion Paper,* London.

THE ROYAL TOWN PLANNING INSTITUTE (1973) *Town Planners and their Future – Implications of Changes in Education and Membership Policy: A Further Discussion Paper,* London.

THE ROYAL TOWN PLANNING INSTITUTE (1974) Education Policy. *The Planner,* Vol. 60: 802-808.

THE TOWN PLANNING INSTITUTE (1971) *One Day Membership Policy Conference,* University of Manchester, 24 February.

YOUNG, M. (1968) Forecasting in the social sciences. *Forecasting in the Social Sciences* (edited by Young, M.). London: Heinemann, pp. 1-36.

Part IV

Synthesis

The last part comprises my inaugural lecture held at Delft University of Technology in 1975.* Naturally, such an occasion gives one reason to reflect upon past developments and to focus one's thoughts upon the future, and this even more so since giving my inaugural lecture coincided with a substantial re-orientation towards a new environment. The lecture therefore reflects basic tenets of my thinking concerning the twin fields of planning theory and education, but at the same time gives evidence of uncertainty about how to apply them in a new situation. Thus, the distinction between substantial and procedural planning theory reappears, as does the notion of the latter as a generic theory underlying all forms of planning. Likewise, the role of rationality as a central methodological principle (comparable to the falsification principle in empirical research) is re-emphasised in a manner which, I would like to think, expresses it more clearly than my earlier work. Finally, the essential link between planning and democracy which exists through its inherent tendency towards a measure of decentralisation receives attention.

However, it is evident that points which the previous essay could make succinctly had to be tuned down. The audience of this inaugural lecture was primarily the Department of Architecture and Town Planning (Bouwkunde) of Delft University of Technology and *not* a group composed only of planners. Whilst being the largest single planning school of sorts in the country (most of the other schools are smaller in size and offer planning specialisation – "*planologie*" – to social scientists and geographers in the final years of their course), Bouwkunde has a strong urban design tradition and has never fully endorsed the view that town planning might

*The Dutch version as given at Delft has been published before by Delft University Press under the title *Planningtheorie en Planningonderwijs*.

157

be something different from architecture. Speaking to this audience, I could therefore not help but bear the disputes between architecture and town planning about areas of mutual overlap in mind. Also, the sheer size of the department, and the concomitant divergence of opinions within it, turn arguments concerning course structure such as those expressed in the previous essays into even more contentious issues than they are elsewhere. My ideas therefore had to be whittled down to the bare minimum, hopefully with generally salutary effects on their applicability in a variety of situations. Thus, I still emphasise procedural planning theory as the integrating idea around which an undergraduate-type course structured on the lines of the generalist-with-a-specialism model and with a heavy element of project teaching, together with a substantial input from other disciplines (in particular from the social sciences) might evolve. But I also recognise parallels between architecture and planning, describing them as examples of Simon's *Sciences of the Artificial* (Simon, 1969). In fact, what this amounts to is that the "generalist-with-a-specialism" logic might be extended even beyond planning in the generic sense in which my essays tend to use this term. One could conceive of courses so broad as to cover all forms of purposive intervention, from architectural design to policy sciences, a thought which is not quite so far-fetched as it might sound coming from a department which spans a field from interior design to national urbanisation policy. Although I do not see much prospect of any such developments occurring in the near future, we cannot exclude the possibility. These contingencies and their implications are what my final remarks over planning education providing models for more general forms of education refer to.

Reference

SIMON, H. A. (1969) *The Sciences of the Artificial*, MIT Press, Cambridge, Mass.

Planning Theory
and the Education of Planners *

Hallstatt is a small village which without its salt-mining tradition would hardly have developed in its very awkward location, perched on a steep slope rising out of one of the beautiful lakes of Upper Austria. So steep is this slope that for a long time access to Hallstatt was mainly across the lake. Wooden boat huts symbolise its links with the water. With the houses huddling together on an enormous mountainside, the spire of the church and the dark woods, these make for an extremely picturesque scene, especially when the water is calm and reflects the view of Hallstatt from the lake.

Having invested in a cable-car nearby, the provincial government decided on some road improvements.[1] The bottleneck was Hallstatt where a number of listed buildings prevented the existing road, with its width of slightly more than two metres, from being "improved". Faced with the choice of either building the road above the village where it would have destroyed the scenery altogether, or along the shore of the lake, the government planners opted for the latter solution. The alternative of driving a tunnel through the mountain behind Hallstatt was ruled out as too expensive from the start. In the wake of building the road along the shore, the boat-huts would have to go.

So convinced were the planners that this was the only reasonable solution that they drew up detailed designs, made compulsory purchases and demolished a hotel in the way of the proposed road, despite public protest against the damage to the picturesque scenery.

The ensuing conflict could never be analysed in terms of "them" and "us". There were shifting coalitions between local people and national groups, between economic interests and government agencies, between the

---

* My thanks are due to the other members of the Planning Theory Group who have contributed greatly in giving me their comments on earlier drafts of this lecture.

[1] For a full presentation of this case see A. Faludi (1970/1) Pluralismus im Planungsprozess, *Informationen der Arbeitsgemeinschaft für interdisziplinäre angewandte Sozialforschung*, Bd.2, S.75-92.

press and politicians, etc. At one stage, the socialist dominated council, the mines and the owner of the hotel to be demolished later were all solidly *for* the road, while its opponents seemed to be lacking in organisation and support. Still, a vote amongst the people of Hallstatt went against the government proposal and delayed its implementation.

Next to the political conflict around the road proposal, there is one other factor worth recording — the emergence of new factual knowledge. The director of the local museum and most ardent opponent of the road could point out a fact which the planners had not taken account of: in 1808 there had been a landslide making the ground just off the shore of the lake where the road would have had to be built on concrete piles very treacherous indeed. Similarly, the technical director of the saltmines (which were interested in getting a road soon, but not necessarily along the shore) pointed out, firstly, that the mountain behind Hallstatt was of solid but soft rock through which it would be cheap and easy to drive a tunnel, and, secondly, that in a similar but faraway case the very considerable ventilation problem of a tunnel designed for motorcars had been reduced by building two one-way tunnels so that the cars themselves would push the polluted air out and thus take care of most of the ventilation.

The planners were not impressed. However, to subdue the opposition to their project, they allowed developers to submit alternatives when it was put out for public tender. Surprisingly, the cheapest offer featured two one-way tunnels with minimum damage to the scenery.

What had happened? Hard-headed businessmen had calculated the risks involved in building a road along the shore and set against them the relative ease with which the tunnel could be built, making use of information which had only emerged during the conflict around the official project. Obviously, the comparison must have gone against the latter. The project which resulted was widely acclaimed as a satisfactory solution to the meshing of traffic requirements with the scenic beauty of Austria's landscape and its picturesque buildings.

What conclusions can be drawn from this case out of many[2] where

[2]Two parallel case-studies in A. Faludi (1970/1) *op. cit.* demonstrate the same difficulty of collecting all the information needed in decision-making. In one case, for instance, some proposed road works along the Danube would have endangered shipping. Nevertheless, it was only as a result of public protest that the state shipping company became involved.

there has been a public outcry resulting from an official project leading to a better plan? Had the planners simply been stupid? Should they have asked "the people" first? Could they have known about a landslide in the distant past; about a recent project in another part of the country? This case occurred long before public participation had become an idea of good currency. Also, what is implied in these questions is that planners should be knowledgeable in all fields relevant to the problems before them. Case studies consistently indicate that planners are far from that, that their proposals are often incomplete, insufficiently researched and not meeting the wishes of the people. Therefore, there is often considerable uncertainty surrounding their work.

As Friend and Jessop in their seminal work[3] have shown, uncertainty in planning concerns the nature of the *environment* and the likely results of proposed action; the desirability of promoting certain *values* at the expense of others; and the intentions of other agencies operating in *related areas of choice*. No amount of substantive research can reduce uncertainties of the latter two types. They require political guidance on the one hand and coordination on the other. Not even the first type of uncertainty is always best dealt with by mounting substantive research. In the case described before, what should the planners have researched into? The awareness of the two decisive technical factors changed the perception of the environment, making the underground seem treacherous and the rock not so unsurmountable a problem. But this awareness *presupposed* knowledge of a highly specialised kind. This the planners did not command, nor could they really have been expected to have it. At the outset, even the best multi-disciplinary team cannot combine *all* the substantive knowledge necessary for solving the more intricate planning problems.

But, instead of working out a plan in much detail, assume the planners had done something else. Assume they had said to everybody right at the beginning: "This is how we see the problem, this is the line which we propose, what do you think?" This they could have done with minimum

[3]J. K. Friend and W. N. Jessop (1969) *Local Government and Strategic Choice*, Tavistock, London. For a Dutch summary of the argument concerning uncertainty see: P. Drewe (1973) *Methoden en technieken van het stedebouwkundig planologisch onderzoek, deel I*, Handleidingen kollege hb42, 1973–1974 Course, Afdeling Bouwkunde, Technische Hogeschool Delft.

effort. No doubt, the uproar would have been the same. But they might have been in a frame of mind to learn, to accept the messages concerning matters of fact and value which they received, to consider their implications. They might have done this based on their awareness of the inevitable limitations of their knowledge, giving them the willingness to "embrace error" as Michael put it.[4] In this spirit, they would have avoided investing into an abortive project and explored alternatives at an early stage instead: as subsequent events showed, a much more reasonable procedure for tackling the problem before them, taking less time to produce a better solution.

This conclusion leads me to the first fundamental point about planning theory: every effort to solve problems involves *substantive* knowledge about the variables involved, and *procedural* knowledge for going about tackling the problem. Naturally, when the problem-solver is a group or an organisation,[5] and even more so when a number of organisations are involved,[5] procedural problems are more tangled. Inevitably, they become political, even where there are only private agencies involved.[6] Planning theory concerns itself with the organisations and procedures of problem-solving and not with substantive matters. Its perennial problem is that there is never all the necessary substantive knowledge concentrated in one mind or in one agency. Even if it were, the amount of detail which was worth knowing about a problem would always exceed the information-handling capacity of the problem-solver, be he an individual or a large multi-disciplinary team. Coping intelligently with the uncertainty caused by information overload and by the lack of guidance as to what represents relevant information is the first step towards tackling substantive problems. In this way, procedural planning theory forms the necessary basis for the application of substantive knowledge without, of course, pre-empting the contribution of the latter.

[4]D. L. Michael (1973) *On Learning to Plan – and Planning to Learn*, Jossey-Bass Publishers, San Francisco-Washington-London.

[5]On building "decision networks" between organisations see: J. K. Friend *et al.* (1974) *Public Planning – the Inter-corporate Dimension*, Tavistock, London.

[6]For an early statement on the political dimension even of private organisations see R. Dahl (1959) Business and Politics, in: R. Dahl *et al.* (Eds.) *Social Science Research on Business: Product and Potential*, Columbia University Press, New York.

One might illustrate the meaning of procedural planning theory, and its distinction from theories providing knowledge concerning the subject matter of planning, by reference to the conventional set of planning fields. I mean the well-nigh universal distinction between economic, social and physical planning. Each of these builds on bodies of substantive knowledge concerning different aspects of reality, some of them considerably refined such as economic theory. In applying these, each type of planning also draws cn procedural knowledge. The division between these two types of knowledge is well documented in the work of Tinbergen who simultaneously draws on theory explaining the operation of the economy, and on a set of precepts for how to arrive at economic policy based on it.[7]

Now, it may seem intuitively obvious that there are similarities between the procedures of planning used in its various fields. After all, problem solving is always done by humans. Why should their strategies be substantially different when they solve different problems? The very fact that we describe their actions with the same term planning (witness the use of this word in the names of institutions concerned with widely divergent problems such as the *Centraal Planbureau*, the *Rijksplanologische Dienst* and the *Sociaal-Cultureel Planbureau*) indicates an analogy.

A review of the literature confirms this similarity. The planning process as presented by Tinbergen is more or less the same as that advocated by Chapin,[8] McLoughlin[9] and Chadwick[10] to name but a few theorists of physical planning, or as by a theorist of social planning such as Kahn.[11] Planning theory deals with those features of the organisations and procedures of planning which are similar in all its field, including their

[7]J. Tinbergen (1964) *Central Planning*, Yale University Press, New Haven; J. Tinbergen (1967) *Development Planning*, Weidenfeld & Nicolson, London.

[8]F. S. Chapin (1965) *Urban Land Use Planning* (2nd Ed.) University of Illinois Press, Urbana, Ill.

[9]J. B. McLoughlin (1969) *Urban and Regional Planning: a Systems Approach*, Faber & Faber, London.

[10]G. Chadwick (1971) *A Systems View of Planning*, Pergamon, Oxford.

[11]A. Kahn (1969) *Theory and Practice of Social Planning*, Russell Sage Foundation, New York.

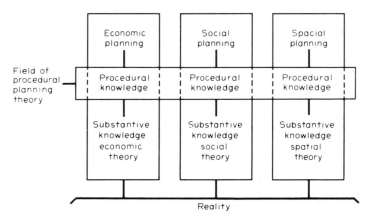

Fig. 1   Procedural and Substantive Knowledge in Planning.

systematic variations (Fig. 1).

What is less obvious but amounts to the second fundamental point of this lecture is that the basic idea underlying these procedures, and of the organisations evolving around them, is that of *rationality*.[12] Rationality in planning means nothing more and nothing less than it does in everyday life. We would never term any action rational to which there was a conceivable alternative which achieved its ends better, just as we were critical of the official project in the case study presented before, because there had been a superior alternative. So, to keep within the somewhat doubtful distinction into three major planning fields, economic planning aims to identify the best mix of monetary and/or investment policies to be pursued, social planning the best approach to providing health, welfare and recreational facilities, and physical planning the best distribution of land uses and communication lines. Each of them has procedures for actively seeking the best course of action through evaluating the consequences of all alternatives against all relevant ends. Rationality is therefore a feature

[12]H. A. Simon (1965) *Administrative Behavior* (2nd Ed.), The Free Press, New York, was written during World War II. For a Dutch translation see: Besluitvorming in de organisatie (1967), J. H. de Bussy, Amsterdam.

of decision processes aiming to identify what best to do in given situations.

This standard of rationality is so simple, and so ingrained in our way of thinking, that there cannot be any reasonable objection against invoking it as a yardstick which we apply every time that we wish to determine whether a particular decision is reasonable. Arguments against rationality do not take issue with it but are mostly of a twofold kind: firstly, it is said that the ends pursued are not the right ones. Secondly, it is argued that rationality, whilst desirable, is impossible to achieve. I shall discuss both and make some further points about the desirability of rationality.

The first argument is advanced in many forms, the most frequent one being that of criticising the ends of particular projects. The closing of the Oosterschelde was criticised not because it was an ineffective way of providing the level of safety stipulated, but because that level of safety was thought to be excessive, and because a complete closure, though it would achieve the ends set for the project, would radically change the environment of the estuary.[13] Thus, a new set of ends was added to the existing ones, ends considered so important that a solution three times as expensive, providing safety much later, was considered superior to the one proposed before.[14]

What does the Oosterschelde case show? The arguments which carried the day were those about what ought to be achieved or avoided. It seems reasonable that changes in the ends pursued should result in a different project. Once the changes in the set of ends were taking shape, new technical knowledge in the form of a new type of dam came to the fore. At present, this dam is being proposed as a solution to the newly conceived problem of giving safety whilst retaining the estuary. The *standards of argument* remain the same, only the *perception of the problem* has changed. (Since this has been written, the argument around

[13]For a useful collection of case material on the Oosterchelde decision see: Vakgroep Civiele Planologie (1973/4) *Veiligheid versus milieu*, Handleiding Kollege e-3, Afdeling Weg- en Waterbouwkunde, Technische Hogeschool Delft. On the excessive level of safety stipulated by the original plan see J. C. Terlouw, Oosterschelde: kraamkamer van de Noordzee (1974) *NRC-Handelsblad*, 16 November.

[14]Since ends form part of problem formulation, one might also say that the problem was now perceived as being more complex requiring a more sophisticated approach, i.e. thinking in terms of alternatives instead of solutions.

the Oosterschelde project has taken two more turns. However, if anything this merely enforces my point: perceptions change, standards of argument remain the same.)

In this case we may detect two forms of rationality which Karl Mannheim[15] has termed functional and substantial respectively. Their difference lies in the scope of the problems to which rationality is being applied. Functional rationality accepts given ends; substantial rationality is concerned with these very ends themselves. Many of the arguments against rational planning can be translated into demands for a more comprehensive, more substantial, form of rationality. But, in the end, solving the problem still means thinking in terms of the consequences of a set of alternatives, and striving for finding the best solution amongst them given an, albeit wider, set of ends.

A variant of the demand for more substantial rationality is the argument that the present economic and political system consistently favours one set of interests and neglects others, and is thus substantially irrational and should be changed. But to sustain the argument one has to *show* that the consequences of the present system are detrimental to some desired set of ends and that its alternatives are not. Thus, one uses the same rational procedure. And, if the substantial irrationality were removed, we would still be faced with making choices which we could only justify by demonstrating that they were superior to their alternatives. The standard of rationality is therefore not at issue.

What does transpire though is the fact that rationality itself, because it leads to thinking in terms of alternatives and their consequences, has a critical potential. It is certainly not inherent to the concept that it should accept given ends and support the existing order of things. This I shall illustrate by drawing on the three levels of feedback as identified by Deutsch[16] and Buckley.[17] Each of these represents one potential entry point into a rational argument for change.

[15]K. Mannheim (1940) *Man and Society in an Age of Reconstruction*, Kegan Paul, London.

[16]K. W. Deutsch (1966) *The Nerves of Government* (2nd Ed.), Macmillan, New York-London.

[17]W. Buckley (1967) *Sociology and Modern Systems Theory*, Englewood Cliffs, New Jersey.

Firstly, there is feedback concerning the achievement of *given* ends. Secondly, there is *goal-changing* feedback which is evident in the Oosterschelde case. Thirdly, there is feedback relating to just the question which radical critics of planning raise: that it consistently favours one particular set of interests. This is feedback concerning how the organisations and procedures of planning themselves affect the outcomes of decisions. Such feedback may result in organisational and procedural changes, what one might term *meta-planning*. The pursuit of rationality in planning always includes meta-planning as a potential option.[18] On this level, nothing precludes us from rationally considering what are often presented as radical solutions, including the redistribution of economic and political power. I am therefore surprised that radicals often show such a distaste for rationality. To my mind, this stems from a too narrow concept of the scope of its application.

Rather than dismissing rationality, radicals should emulate the example set by Cornforth in his critique of Popper's anti-Marxism.[19] Cornforth claims that Popper's position is unreasonable by his own standards of rationality, and that there are perfectly rational arguments for Marxist policies. Without going into the matter, I can of course make no pronouncements about the reasonableness of this critique. I merely invoke the example to illustrate my point that there are, in fact, no *a priori* limits to the scope of problems to which rationality might be applied.

Of course, whether radical solutions are in fact needed, or whether their disadvantages outweigh their advantages (in particular in view of the uncertainty which often surrounds them) depends on the case at hand. Rationality might thus provide a check on dogmatic radicalism, which is all to the best since dogmatism is always harmful from wherever it comes. But otherwise radicalism has the potential of extending the scope of rational problem-solving, and rationality supports the need for radical analysis. Properly conceived, they can go hand in hand.

---

[18]On meta-planning as one aspect of the "problem of planning theory" see A. Faludi (1973) *Planning Theory*, Pergamon, Oxford. For a much more elaborate treatment of meta-planning see Y. Dror (1968) *Public Policymaking Reexamined*, Chandler, Scranton, Pa.

[19]M. Cornforth (1968) *The Open Philosophy and the Open Society*, Lawrence & Wishart, London.

Criticisms of the ends pursued in planning, or of the way in which it is conducted, therefore do not invalidate the principle of rational decision-making in planning. What might very well invalidate it is the argument that it is *not in fact possible* to make decisions rationally. More precisely, it is argued that it is impossible to identify all courses of action open to a decision-maker and to evaluate their consequences against all relevant ends. The truth of this statement is as obvious as it is deceptive. I shall concentrate on one aspect of this critique: on the claim that one cannot explore all alternatives. With my example I hope to demonstrate how unreasonable the critics of rationality are in insisting to apply the prescriptions of rational decision-making to the letter rather than taking account of the situations in which human beings act.

Let us see how rationality works in everyday life. Cycling home along the Mekelweg on a dark winter evening, I pass the bank at the corner outside this lecture hall. I do not normally consider the alternative of getting off the bike, smashing the windows and attempting to rob the bank. Now, it would certainly be possible in principle to do so. Thanks to films and television, we all have some rudimentary knowledge of how one robs a bank. However, I do not even consider this course of action. Am I therefore not rational? Is the thug who does consider this alternative, and who subsequently sets out to implement his plan, more rational than I am? The common-sense answer is of course that these are meaningless questions, that being a professor excludes courses of action such as robbing banks which might be rational for thugs. Thus, in everyday life we accept that there is a *context* within which decisions are made, and that being rational means choosing from among a certain limited number of alternatives within that context. By disregarding this very simple and commonly accepted fact, the critics of rational planning have built a strawman of an omnipotent rational planner which, sure enough, they succeed in knocking down.

Rationality is thus *contextual*. But what is that context? Obviously, in the Oosterschelde case this was not as easy to decide as it is for me on a dark evening outside the bank. Under the onslaught of new arguments based on new insights and new ways of thinking, the context of the Oosterschelde decision has changed from the time when the Delta-legislation was enacted to the current cabinet decision. But changes in the context of planning do not invalidate the point made earlier that there are limits to the number of alternatives considered. For instance, nobody seems to argue that present levels of safety are adequate. Despite the fact that there were no similar occurrences in the more than twenty years since the catastrophic spring-tide of 1953, the alternative of leaving things as they are is therefore excluded.

What becomes evident about the context of rational planning though is that there is often uncertainty about where actual feasibility lies. It is thus reasonable that the context should occasionally become the object of rational argument in turn. We are back to where we ended the discussion about ends in planning. Summarising the argument we may say now that feasible rational planning occurs in an envelope of substantive, normative and procedural assumptions. Initially, it aims at making the best choices within that context. Occasionally it gives rise to arguments questioning that context in turn, arguments which often lead to change.

So this argument against rational planning cannot be sustained. Nor can others about the limited calculatory power of humans to perform simultaneous evaluations of alternatives. Firstly, this varies from case to case, and progress towards better evaluation, even of so-called intangibles, seems possible. Secondly, much as contextual ones, human limitations can of course be taken account of in a perfectly rational manner.[20] So rationality emerges unscathed as what it is: a standard which reasonable people invoke in evaluating their decisions.

But are there also positive arguments for engaging in rational planning? Firstly and most obviously there is the fact that it helps in finding better solutions to the problems before us. Secondly, knowing what the alternatives and their consequences are, is also the best way of making responsible political decisions. Thirdly, the attempt to plan rationally results in learning. The first point has been given ample coverage in the case-study at the beginning. The second and third warrant further consideration.

In his recent inaugural lecture, Herman van Gunsteren concerned himself with the nature of political responsibility.[21] He claims that it can

[20]J. G. March and H. A. Simon (1958) Taking account of human limitations, *Organizations*, John Wiley, New York, propose to replace the optimising criterion with the less demanding satisficing rule.

[21]H. R. van Gunsteren (1974) *Denken over politieke verantwoordelijkheid*, Samsom, Alphen aan de Rijn.

only be determined through people in concrete situations talking to each other. With this, he describes how political responsibility is formed. But he leaves out the rules for deciding whether a decision is responsible. Rational planning provides the grammar for saying whether the decision-maker has discharged his responsibility properly. This presupposes what I previously identified as the most central feature of planning: thinking in terms of the consequences of alternative courses of action for a set of ends, often leading to thinking about alternative sets of ends in turn. Without thinking in such terms, political decisions remain blind to some or most of their real effects and to their opportunity costs. Thus, political responsibility cannot be shouldered without planning.

It is often said that planning is politics which is of course true. But it now transpires that responsible politics must also be planning. Similar points have been made by Kuypers[22] and Nagel,[23] but the political scientists recognising this symmetry are rather an exception. The symmetry of politics and planning gives a rationale to the latter. Planning should enable politicians to take political decisions in a political way,[24] i.e. knowing and accepting all their consequences.

The example of the Oosterschelde shows that the critical potential of rational planning referred to earlier applies not only to the ends pursued, but also to closely related questions of fact: how much damage would be done to estuary life, to life in the ocean; is it technically possible to build a dam which prevents this damage; how much would it cost? This is an illustration of the learning effect of attempting to plan rationally. Learning is an important consequence of, and an independent argument for, rational planning, as can be seen in cases where projects have been abandoned.

Take Maplin, the third London airport now abandoned by the British government. Has all the effort put into the preparation of the decision been futile because it resulted in no action? I would deny this. In my submission, there have been benefits in terms of increased awareness of the

---

[22]G. Kuypers (1973) *Grondbegrippen van politiek*, Uitgeverij Het Spectrum, Utrecht/Antwerpen.

[23]A. Nagel (1973) *Politische Entscheidungslehre*, Dissertationsdruck, Universität Heidelberg.

[24]M. Teschner (1969) at a discussion on planning education organised by the Akademie für Städtebau und Landesplanung in Munich.

problems and external costs of air traffic, of the procedures to be used in making important decisions, of the "nonsense on stilts", as Peter Self expressed it,[25] of trying to make such decisions based purely on a cost-benefit approach, and in terms of public awareness of the frailty of many assumptions underlying capital projects. Having demonstrated these points is no mean achievement and could have considerable impact on the future conduct of planning.[26]

Learning never ends. Learning even seems to accelerate. It is not subject to the law of entropy, except in the very general sense that when the universe fades out of existence, learning will also come to an end. Certainly, for the present and foreseeable future we may anticipate the spread of learning, not the least because the number of people sharing in the planning-cum-learning process increases. It is indeed no exaggeration to say that more and more people in practice participate in planning. Military staffs were the first planners and, though we may regret their purpose, there is something to be learned from them about decision-making under uncertainty and pressure of time. The separation of ownership and management in industry, the emergence of a career-executive, the formation of staff-planning units in public and private bureaucracies all over the world, they all bear witness to the same growing emphasis on planning.

There are also good, theoretical reasons for spreading planning outside the staff-units where it is usually practised. As demonstrated in the case of the road proposal, it is impossible to centralise all the knowledge which is essential for good planning. Consequently, planning theory suggests that planning should fuse with all kinds of societal decision-making. Good planning decentralises decision-making. For instance, the military example teaches that armies which execute plans conceived by their general staffs with great care and exactitude may thereby commit errors.[27] Reputedly flexible armies do not narrowly prescribe the actions of individual units. On the contrary, their organisation and training aim at spreading the capa-

[25]P. Self (1970), Nonsense on stilts, *New Society*, 2 July.

[26]One can only hazard a guess as to whether the decision to expand Schiphol or to build a second Dutch national airport will be influenced by the demise of Maplin.

[27]Sunday Times Insight Team (1974) *Insight on the Middle East War*, André Deutsch, London.

bility of making decisions within a framework of strategic goals.[28] Large industrial firms are likewise not run from the top. For some time now, management science is endorsing the view that decisions should be made as far down the line as possible, ideally where their consequences must be borne.[29] Corporate planning units in public authorities, rather than becoming the super-brain trusts as which they were often perceived by their opponents, tend to be small and view it as their main task to induce existing departments to adopt planning. In economic planning, even of a Socialist genre, we are also a long way off from the early vision of the whole of a society being guided by a central plan, just as an army or a corporation supposedly is.[30] Even wartime economic planning demonstrates the supremacy, irrespective of ideology, of decentralised planning within some broad form of coordination.[31] In short, everywhere we witness the devolution of planning away from the centre and its spread throughout society.

This tendency does not stop at institutional boundaries. Planners are seeking to establish partnerships with the people. Often, this is interpreted as the advocacy of the interests of disadvantaged groups. However, it is worth remembering that Paul Davidoff coining the term advocacy planner in 1965 also linked it with the improvement of the overall rationality of planning through making it more representative of the pluralism in the community at large.[32] I therefore see a second, independent source for

[28]D. Young (1967) *The Israeli Campaign 1967*, William Kimber, London.

[29]"Classical theory states that decisions should be assigned to the lowest competent level in the organisation, which is an excellent rule so far as it goes. The closer a decision-maker is to the scene of action, the quicker the decision can be made. And, of course, if too many decisions are passed up the line, higher executives will be overburdened and those in the lower echelons will have little opportunity to use initiative." E. Dale (1965) *Management: Theory and Practice*, McGraw-Hill, New York.

[30]On these early visions, see B. Gross (1971), Changing styles of planning, *Public Administration Review*, Vol. 31, pp. 265-97. On the influence which the German military theorist Von Clausewitz had on Lenin's thinking see Kuypers (1973), *op. cit.*

[31]E. Devons (1970) *Papers on Planning and Economic Management*, Manchester University Press, Manchester, on English, and A. Speer (1969) *Erinnerungen*, Propyläen, Berlin, on German wartime planning.

[32]P. Davidoff (1965), Advocacy and pluralism in planning, *Journal of the American Institute of Planners*, Vol. 31, pp. 331-8.

the movement towards participatory, or advocacy, planning which does not conflict with, but even enforces the concern for equality: the concern for overall rationality in planning.

So I see planning spreading in practice. I see *ad hoc* planning groups springing up, neighbourhood planning centres, planning "clinics", planning games on community television, and of course much more decision-making on lower levels than is thought conceivable at present. Planning theory explains and promotes this spread by demonstrating the impossibility in principle of central planning in any real sense of the word. It does this by pointing out the information-handling requirements of such an enterprise on the one hand,[33] and the limited capacity of any decision-maker, whether an individual or a collective, of simultaneously assessing information on the other. From this it deduces the likelihood of utter harm being done by over-zealous central planning. The need for decentralisation and for other than coercive means for whatever control must remain centralised follows.[34]

Naturally, I view the spread of planning sketched out before with some pleasure. However, there is unease creeping in. Clearly, my present efforts aim at establishing planning theory as a discipline. Discipline implies something distinct. Discipline means pursuing a definite purpose, using a number of clearly defined terms and models, and having research findings which one may call one's own. But, if the vision of planning becoming the accepted way of conducting our affairs were to become true, this would tend to erode its distinctive character. A planning society would never regard planning as a task purely for experts. But with planning losing its distinct character, planning theory too would tend to lose some of its identity. Advocates of planning already tend to get involved in pretty much everything, and in particular the most important issue of institution building. They are potential constitution builders, as Herman van

[33]R. Bićanić (1967) *Problems of Planning — East and West*, Mouton, Den Haag, quotes the figure of 90 million "norms" which were supposed to be issued centrally in the Soviet Union.

[34]The move towards decentralisation and less coercive means of control is reflected in the development of Dutch national physical planning. The Planning Theory Group hopes to study this development in future. For a first attempt see P. de Ruijter (1975) *De Rijksplanologische Dienst*, Working Papers in Planning Theory and Education, No. 5. Vereniging voor Studi — en Studentenbelangen te Delft.

Gunsteren[35] pointed out so aptly. The role of planners in, for example, the reform of local government bears witness to the truth of his contention. However, constitution-building is of eminent practical concern for every mature citizen. Thus, with the advent of a planning society, planning theory might become something much less clearly defined than an academic discipline. Right at the end, I shall make a similar point about planning education. By merging with other kinds of education for practice, it too might become less distinct than at present.

But first we must examine the role of procedural planning theory in planning education as offered at Bouwkunde, for example. Here comes my last fundamental point today: that the future development, in particular of the early parts, of our course would be assisted by more explicit attention to organisational and procedural matters. I said more *explicit* because, obviously, organisations and procedures *are* being dealt with throughout the course. Making this explicit would allow us to determine where the balance of emphasis should lie in every part of the course and to express more clearly how the parts of the curriculum hang together.

My starting point is that Bouwkunde partakes in spatial planning. With other planning fields, spatial planning shares its assumptions about how to plan. But its subject matter is of course different from that of either economic or social planning. In adapting this subject matter to human needs, spatial planning might draw on urban and regional theory, knowledge of the technical processes by which the environment is changed, etc. The need to cover these at Bouwkunde is not at issue. I can even envisage some more emphasis on what is often termed "the new geography", especially if Bouwkunde wishes to expand its regional planning activities.

The question to ask though is where a planning course draws its identity from. Based on the deceptively obvious principle that planning must be based on thorough acquaintance with what is being planned, there is a tendency in planning education to rely too much on substantive knowledge.

Since I am going to propose an alternative to this subject-matter

[35]H. van Gunsteren (1974), Planning en politiek, *Bestuurswetenschappen*, Vol. 28, pp. 27-48, en Politiek nieuws van het planningsfront, *Politisering van het openbaar bestuur*, Congresuitgave Vereniging voor Bestuurškunde, Uitgeverij van Nederlandse Gemeenten, 's-Gravenhage.

orientated view of planning education, I should point out that it is not only the most widespread view, but also has good arguments on its side. Its holders can point to the educational value of acquiring a basic discipline before engaging in the tricky business of prescription.[36] Another line of argument says with some justification that planning requires a well-rounded personality, and that it is, therefore, only suitable for advanced courses for people who have exercised their minds in acquiring a disciplinary base. In yet a further variant, the argument goes that planning must be learned "on the job", and that substantive knowledge is all that could be taught.

However, the subject-matter based approach to planning education suffers from the crucial problem that "God did not see fit to distribute problems in accordance with university chairs".[37] The usual response is that of providing a multi-disciplinary base for planning. Bouwkunde therefore has a very respectable range of disciplines on its staff, and the courses in *planologie* accept people from a number of social-science disciplines.

Unfortunately, there are problems with the multidisciplinary approach too. However comprehensive the range of disciplines, important areas of knowledge may still be left out. Also, multidisciplinary planning education ducks the central question of what planning is. In a multidisciplinary course, by definition, there is no core discipline and thus no intellectual backbone around which to integrate learning and teaching.

The problem is not at all unique to planning education. To name but a few, architecture, engineering, management, public administration and social work seem to experience similar problems in shaping an educational curriculum. In each of these fields, the curriculum is being expanded through the accretion of disciplines purporting to provide the scientific basis for what they are doing. Sometimes this results in an identity crisis over the question of what the intellectual core of these fields is, over and

[36]In recent discussions around the formation of an Interfacultaire Werkgroep Technische Planologie, this position also came to the fore. See P. de Haan (1974) *Nota betreffend instelling interfaculteit voor technische planologie*, Mimeo, Technische Hogeschool Delft. P. Hall (1973), Manpower and education, *The Future of Planning*, Heinemann, London, suggest three basic disciplines, two of which are substantive: cybernetics, geography, economics.

[37]Contribution to a conference discussion quoted in A. Cherns *et al.* (Eds.), (1972) *Social Science and Government*, Tavistock, London.

above the knowledge provided by other disciplines.[38]

This is not where the similarity ends. These fields also have their action-orientation in common. Their interest in various other disciplines is but a derivative of their concern with practical ends. They are therefore not interested in knowledge *per se* but in harnessing whatever knowledge is needed to achieve these ends. Because they invariably involve the design of new, and to this extent artificial situations, Simon describes them as *The Sciences of the Artificial.*[39]

These "sciences of the artificial" are developing their common language and approaches. Ends, alternatives, choices, uncertainty and decision-maker are universal categories of any discourse about intervention. Methods like linear programming are widely used. Analysis of Interconnected Decision Areas (AIDA), once developed to aid architectural design,[40] is now being applied to structure planning.[41] Planning programming budgeting developed by the American Defence Department currently provides an approach to coordination and budgeting in local authorities, in the Netherlands,[42] amongst other places.

Of course we must not stretch the claim for universal usefulness too far. These general approaches must necessarily be amplified during application. Decision makers must always have substantive knowledge, and a good deal of feel for the situation they are in as well (what Friedmann terms personal knowledge).[43] But the general knowledge, skills and attitudes

---

[38]This crisis is aggravated in the case of relatively young professions having to draw on the services of academically more respectable disciplines. See N. Glazer (1974), Conflicts in schools for the minor professions, *Minerva: A Review of Science, Learning and Policy*, Vol. 10, pp. 346-64.

[39]H. A. Simon (1969) *The Sciences of the Artificial*, MIT Press, Cambridge, Mass.

[40]J. Luckman (1967), An approach to the management of design, *Operational Research Quarterly*, Vol. 18, pp. 345-58.

[41]J. Friend (1974) *Conjectures on Policy-Making*, Mimeo, Institute for Operational Research, Coventry.

[42]J. P. de Looff and G. M. Kersten (1972) *Grondslagen voor een geïntegreerd gemeentelijk bestuurssysteem (GGBS)*, IBW Reeks nr.20, Uitgeverij van Nederlandse Gemeenten, 's-Gravenhage.

[43]J. Friedmann (1973) *Retracking America: a Theory of Transactive Planning*, Doubleday, New York.

needed in designing courses of action to achieve practical ends must form part of any educational programme preparing for practice nevertheless.

Within the spectrum of disciplines named as being concerned with design in this very wide sense of the term, spatial planning has a special place, due to the context in which most spatial planners work on the one hand and the architectural tradition of planning education on the other. The context in which the spatial planner operates brings him more and more into the field of policy making; his architectural heritage gives him a uniquely action-oriented education through project work. I shall elaborate on both these points.

Spatial planners working in the public sphere are in constant touch with various technical and administrative experts, politicians and members of the public. Their work is circumscribed by the law, by administrative procedures, budgets, grants, etc. Every one of their proposals may quickly turn into a political issue, so they must have a thorough appreciation of public affairs, and of how organisations and procedures affect the design of policies. The systematic process of designing policies in a public setting we may term the *planning process*.

Mastery of this planning process should be a central objective of planning education. Students must also know about *roles* in the planning process, i.e. their own future role as mostly bureaucratic experts, as well as that of others. They must know about how these roles are arranged, i.e. they must have an understanding of planning organisations. Roles and organisations in turn are set in a *context*. Here, students must have a thorough knowledge of the constitutional and legal systems of their own country, its administrative set-up, assumptions underlying, etc. They must also be aware of likely changes in this context, i.e. its dynamics. They must finally learn how particular types of context circumscribe the very effectiveness of planning. This narrows the area of concern under the context of planning to those factors determining the ability of planning agencies to plan rationally, what I once termed the planning environment.[44] (See Fig. 2.)

Where does this leave substantive knowledge? It still represents a firm basis for solving planning problems. But, in early years in any case, the

[44] A. Faludi (1970), The planning environment and the meaning of "planning", *Regional Studies*, Vol. 4, pp. 1-9.

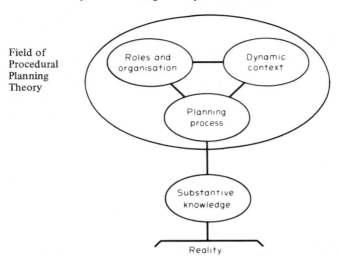

Field of
Procedural
Planning
Theory

Fig. 2   Areas of Concern of Planning Education

acquisition of substantive knowledge would not be an end in itself. If, as Paul Drewe pointed out in this lecture hall some months ago,[45] the exact requirements of practice cannot be anticipated by more than two or three years, then there is not much point in orienting the early years of planning education towards the substantive problems of practice anyway. So, the acquisition of substantive knowledge would mainly serve two purposes: firstly, for learning about planning one clearly has to explore how it solves substantive problems. Substantive knowledge would thus form an essential basis for doing what a planning course ought to concentrate on: learning about planning. Secondly, whilst acquiring substantive knowledge, students would also practice learning. From a planning theoretical point of view I would even say that, whatever substantive knowledge they do acquire, they should preferably have to do so under pressure of time. Limitation of time is one of the most significant features of planning practice and makes the greatest demands on the planner's ability of

[45]P. Drewe (1974) *Stedebouwkundig planologisch onderzoek – onderzoek waarvoor?*, Delftse Universitaire Pers, Delft.

learning rapidly and purposively about the situations he is dealing with. Thus, learning must occur under pressure, but without prejudice to periods of leisurely reflection. I shall turn to how I see the conditions for this being established in planning education when dealing with project work.

In later years of a planning course substantive knowledge has a somewhat different role. Here, there is a reasonable chance of gearing learning and teaching more closely to practice, simply because the time-lag between learning something and applying it in practice is shorter. Also, with the prospect of planning practice before them, students can only gain from applying themselves to a substantive area of concern which they feel strongly about. The planning process, having been ingrained in the students' minds before, can now recede into the background.

Needless to say that there are implications of my view about the roles of procedural and substantive knowledge in terms of an emphasis on planning theory, as well as on approaches and techniques relating to individual phases of the planning process. This may sound like a take-over bid, which is not what is intended. As emphasised before, there are procedural aspects to all kinds of planning. Therefore, every planner commands knowledge about planning procedure. The planning theorist depends on this first-hand experience, reflects upon it, puts it into context. Better still for a teaching situation, he induces others to engage in reflection through dialogue.

Next to a thorough appreciation of the planning process, and of the techniques used in it, planning involves skills which are far less tangible and far more difficult to learn, but which I am sure those involved in projects at Bouwkunde already acquire. I mean the willingness to take risks, the ability to seek out and reformulate relevant information, to synthesise data from different sources, to anticipate reactions from other people, to build coalitions around a project so as to safeguard its implementation, in short, the skills which make a good practitioner.[46]

[46] On these skills see amongst others: J. Bellush and M. Hausknecht (1966), Entrepreneurs and urban renewal, *Journal of the American Institute of Planners*, Vol. 32, pp. 289-97; H. Gamberg (1966), The professional and policy choices in middle-sized cities, *Journal of the American Institute of Planners*, Vol. 32, pp. 174-7; J. Friedmann (1973) *op. cit.*; J. K. Friend *et al.* (1974) *op. cit.*; L. E. Susskind (1974), The logic of planning practice: a new focus for the teaching of planning theory, *Symposium on Planning Theory*, Co-sponsored by the Association of Collegiate Schools of Planning and the American Institute of Planners, Denver, Colorado.

Because of the difficulty of defining, describing, teaching and testing them, it is often said that these must be learned in practice. My view is that, in project work, planning education has a way of teaching them, and that it is this strength on which we should build. I say this with a deep bow to our mother discipline, architecture, from whom we have inherited the aptitude for project teaching. I am certain it gives us an edge of advantage over other types of education struggling to establish project work with little time left for it in the curriculum and sometimes even less inclination on part of the majority of staff to engage in this alien form of teaching.[47]

Now, this emphasis on project work might sound rather mundane. Projects in planning education often show a crude realism trying to ape the end product of a practical project without being able to simulate the conditions under which same product would emerge in practice. These conditions, i.e. the roles to be assumed by planning students, the organisational context, and how feedback is to be obtained, must form part of every project brief. The absence of such information often leads to justifiable complaints about lack of realism.[48]

Social scientists in planning education sometimes puzzle about the usefulness of the extraordinary amount of time spent by students bent over the drawing board.[49] On the other hand, project work is being advanced as a new approach to making learning and teaching more meaningful by educationalists, some of them with a radical inclination.[50] With proper care, project work can indeed be turned into a flexible instrument creating learning and teaching situations (including role playing

[47]On the problems see the classic of planning education, H. S. Perloff (1957) *Education for Planning – City, State and Regional*, John Hopkins, Baltimore.

[48]G. Crispin (1975) *Project Work in Education for Urban and Regional Planning*, Working Papers in Planning Theory and Education, No. 4, Vereniging voor Studie- en Studentenbelangen te Delft.

[49]E. Reade (1972) Sociology in planning education, *Official Architecture and Planning*, Vol. 35, pp. 783-4.

[50]B. Bernstein (1971) On the classification and framing of educational knowledge, *Knowledge and Control* by M. F. D. Young (Ed.), Collier Macmillan, London, pp. 47-69, deals with project work as a vehicle for integrating curricula but never refers to project work in architectural and planning education.

exercises, gaming, etc.) where students apply knowledge to some purpose, get feedback, and subsequently think about their experiences, strengths and weaknesses. With this students may form what is to my mind the most essential ingredient of success in practice: reflectiveness. From reflectiveness, most other features of good practice knowledge flow.[51] Reflectiveness allows one to see things in context, to step outside one's own situation and slip into the shoes of others, to think out possible implications of what one does, not only in a purely analytic sense but using one's imagination to supplement hard knowledge.

I therefore plead with you to advance project work as the central vehicle of planning education. There can be many different kinds of projects, and nobody needs to think that his project would have no place in a future curriculum. The only thing I am saying is that discussion about project work is essential and should be promoted so as to improve upon its conduct. If my lecture does just that, then it will have served its purpose.

Although it would be the central learning and teaching vehicle to convey the knowledge, skills and attitudes needed for planning, including the requisite reflectiveness about oneself and one's role in society, project work does not exhaust what I have to say about the planning curriculum. The other strength of planning education is that planning courses can usually offer their students a variety of disciplinary inputs. The presence of representatives from many disciplines offers opportunities, complaints about the lack of integration of their teaching notwithstanding. It is again in project work that they should find an arena within which to formulate ideas about the relevance of their disciplines to planning. This might have innumerable advantages for their course work. They could quote more planning examples, build links with projects and develop a language common with their planning colleagues. In this way, project work might act as a socialising agent for staff. According to Bernstein,[52] socialisation of staff is indeed a pre-requisite of meaningfully integrated teaching.

To summarise my points as regards the planning curriculum, a course might look as follows. Firstly, there would be projects, case studies,

---

[51]H. D. Lasswell (1971) *A Pre-view of Policy Sciences*, American Elsevier, New York, expresses this idea in terms of the distinction between contemplation and manipulation in policy science.

[52]B. Bernstein (1971) *op. cit.*

courses, etc., dealing directly with aspects of planning and forming the backbone of the curriculum. Initially, they would concentrate on conveying an understanding of the planning process,[53] subsequently exploring its application in a variety of situations and making progressively more use of the range of staff at Bouwkunde so as to give planning students experience in working with representatives of other disciplines.

So much for the core curriculum. In terms of multidisciplinary input I envisage three types. Firstly, there would be basic courses in each of the disciplines aiming to explain their approaches and their relevance to planning, ideally using a case-study approach to elucidate the latter. Secondly, I see more advanced courses on the application of these disciplines to planning based on a firm common idea about what planning is. Lastly, representatives of all disciplines might participate in one or more advanced seminars concerned with issues on the frontiers of planning knowledge.[54]

The appropriate form of the latter must still be developed. But the fact that I said representatives of all disciplines should participate emphasises that I see the core of planning knowledge being developed jointly by those concerned. This last type of seminar is thus designed to fuse the core curriculum with its multidisciplinary envelope in continuous dialogue.

This brings me to my last point. Assume the programme before you to be successful sometime in the future, and the role of the planning theorist in planning education might become much less distinct. We might perhaps retain no more of a differentiation than that between relatively more theoretically oriented people on the one hand and people concerned with the application of same theory on the other, just as other disciplines have their "theorists" and "practitioners".

As an afterthought, planning education itself might lose its separate identity and merge with education generally. Firstly, this might be caused

---

[53]A project aiming at conveying these notions has been developed by the Planning Theory Group. See also: Planning Theory Group (1974) *Rational Planning Manual*, Afdeling der Bouwkunde Technische Hogeschool Delft.

[54]Seminars as the backbone of an advanced teaching programme are being experimented with by the Planning Theory Group. See: Planning Theory Group (1974) *Experiences, Ideas, Intentions: A Report of the First Six Months*, Afdeling der Bouwkunde, Technische Hogeschool Delft.

by the spread of planning throughout society, referred to before, making planning into an essential part of general education.[55] Secondly, by concentrating on problem-solving and the capacity to learn in politically-loaded situations and by developing project work which is tailor-made for that purpose, planning education could become a model for education in an increasingly complex, increasingly educated, and increasingly concerned society.

The prospect gives me quite ambivalent feelings. Being concerned with planning education as, at present, a very special type of thing, and with planning theory as part of its emergent core, I am quite uncertain about what my role in that future educational context could be.

Ladies and gentlemen! Maybe this uncertainty also reflects the fact that I am away from the environment of my upbringing and intellectual growth. Undeniably, living abroad gives me great satisfaction. But on days like this, one feels vulnerable in my kind of situation. I cannot thank my teachers as would be customary. The friends of my student days are not in this hall. My former colleagues are also absent and, in any case, what should they say? Their language is different from the one in which I speak to you, and some of the points which I culled from the Dutch context they would find hard to appreciate. One feels somewhat exposed in this situation and becomes more sensitive to the uncertainties of life.

But, of course, the risk is not at all one-sided. In deciding to get involved with me, you have taken as adventurous a step as I have in coming here. However, since my coming, we have made good progress in learning to know each other. I must thank you for the spirit in which you are receiving me and thank you for your attention.

---

[55]Such ideas are currently *en vogue* in Britain. See: Centre for Environmental Studies (1974) *Education for Urban Governance*, Conference Paper 10, London. The Town and Country Planning Association issues a newsletter on "environmental education" in secondary schools. Most recently, the University of Sheffield has been offering courses for local councillors.

URBAN AND REGIONAL PLANNING SERIES

Other Titles in the Series